CLOUDSTREET

Adapted by Nick Enright and Justin Monjo

from the novel by Tim Winton

Current Theatre Series
Currency Press • Sydney
in association with
Company B Belvoir and Black Swan Theatre

CURRENT THEATRE SERIES

First published in 1999 by
Currency Press Ltd,
PO Box 2287
Strawberry Hills NSW 2012
enquiries@currency.com.au
www.currency.com.au
in association with
Company B Belvoir and Black Swan Theatre

Reprinted 1999, 2001

NATIONAL LIBRARY OF AUSTRALIA CIP DATA
Enright, Nick, 1950–.
   Cloudstreet; the play.
   ISBN 0 86819 589 8
   I. Enright, Nicholas, 1950–. II. Monjo, Justin. III. Winton, Tim, 1960–
   Cloudstreet. IV. Company B at Belvoir Street Theatre (Sydney, N.S.W.). V. Black Swan Theatre Company. VI. Title.
   (Series: Current theatre series).
A822.3

Set by Dean Nottle
Printed by Southwood Press, Marrickville.

Contents

ADAPTORS' NOTES

THE ADAPTATION

The idea for this play began with Justin Monjo, who had adapted another Winton novel, *That Eye the Sky*, with Richard Roxburgh for a Sydney production in 1994, which subsequently toured Australia. Justin invited Nick to work on this adaptation, on which we embarked in 1996. We had great help and encouragement at every stage of the process. Neil Armfield and his creative team were our constant and generous collaborators; indeed the design and staging approach evolved in tandem with the text, before, during and after a two-week workshop in May 1997, in which we also drew on the advice and participation of a remarkable company of actors, some of whom later formed the nucleus of the original cast. From this workshop emerged the present three-act shape of the piece. The text underwent further development in rehearsal in the last months of 1997. The present text incorporates new cuts and changes which we have made in preparation for the 1999 tour. We thank all those who have worked with us at every stage, especially Douglas Hedge, who made an exhaustive synopsis of the book and guided us through the early stages of adaptation. Tim Winton showed us around Perth, then left us to our work. We thank him not only for his astonishing novel, but for trusting us to do our best by it.

THE TEXT

Tim Winton's novel is idiosyncratic in punctuation and spelling, mostly in its unerringly idiomatic reflection of ordinary patterns of speech. Readers of novel and play will notice that much of the play's dialogue is lifted from the pages of the book; but here we have mostly been more conventional in matters of punctuation and spelling, in order to provide a clearer and simpler text for actors.

Nick Enright and Justin Monjo

Cloudstreet was first produced by Company B Belvoir and Black Swan Theatre in Berth 9, Darling Harbour, Sydney, on 3 January 1998, with the following cast:

Anna Brockway	HATTIE LAMB / TED'S GIRL / LUCY WENTWORTH / PANSY MULLET
Max Cullen	SAM PICKLES
Judi Farr	ORIEL LAMB / MRS TISBORNE
Julie Forsyth	RED LAMB / BARMAID / DARLEEN / ANTHEA
John Gaden	LESTER LAMB
Claire Jones	ROSE PICKLES
John Leary	LON LAMB / TOBY RAVEN / WOGGA MCBRIDE
Simon Lyndon	TED PICKLES / GERRY CLAY / FRED BLUNT / HEADLEY
Kris McQuade	DOLLY PICKLES / ALMA
Rebecca Massey	ELAINE LAMB / MRS CLAY / MERLE / MEREDITH
Christopher Pitman	QUICK LAMB
Steve Rodgers	CHUB PICKLES / DOCTOR / ANGRY FATHER / BOB / MR WENTWORTH / SARGE
Kevin Smith	BLACK MAN / AMERICAN PILOT / BILL
Daniel Wyllie	FISH LAMB

Director, Neil Armfield
Set Design, Robert Cousins
Costume Design, Tess Schofield
Lighting Design, Mark Howett
Sound Design, Gavin Tempany
Music, Iain Grandage
Choroegrapher, Kate Champion
Assistant Director, Anatoly Frusin
Assistant Designer, Georgina Yabsley

CHARACTERS

THE LAMB FAMILY:

> LESTER
> ORIEL
> FISH
> QUICK
> HATTIE (HAT)
> RED
> ELAINE
> LON

THE PICKLES FAMILY:

> DOLLY
> SAM
> ROSE
> TED
> CHUB

BLACK MAN
[American] PILOT, in Geraldton
COUSIN FRED, at Margaret River
DOCTOR, consulted about FISH
WOGGA MCBRIDE, QUICK's schoolmate
GERRY CLAY
MRS CLAY
SALLY, barmaid at DOLLY's local
DRINKERS at the pub
MARY, TED's first girlfriend
FATHER of a girl impregnated by TED
MR WENTWORTH
LUCY WENTWORTH
MRS TISBORNE, at Baird's
ALMA, telephonist at Baird's
DARLEEN, at Baird's
MERLE, at Baird's
TOBY RAVEN
HEADLEY, of the Poetry Prize committee
MEREDITH, TOBY's literary friend
PANSY MULLET, LON's finacée, then wife
SARGE, QUICK's boss at the Nedlands Police Station
GUESTS at the Dalkeith literary party
LAWYER (perhaps voice only)
MINISTER (perhaps voice only)

PART ONE

PROLOGUE

The Company assemble on stage.

DOLLY: Will you look at us by the river! The whole restless mob of us on spread blankets in the dreamy briny sunshine skylarking and chiacking about for one day, one clear, clean, sweet day in a good world in the midst of our living.

SCENE 1

Margaret River. A lantern is lit. The LAMB FAMILY *huddle around it.*

ORIEL: I think that's done it.

> LESTER *and* ORIEL LAMB *have brought their family—*QUICK, HATTIE, ELAINE, RED, FISH *and* LON—*for a sunset prawning expedition.* QUICK *unravels a prawn net.* LESTER *strips to his underwear to go into the water.*

Red, Elaine, you get some wood. Hattie, you stay and look after Lon.

> RED *drags* ELAINE *off.* HATTIE *takes* LON *for a cuddle.*

LESTER: I'll take the boys.

ORIEL: They're not tall enough.

LESTER: The girls grizzle too much. Drives me mad.

ORIEL: Put on your shoes or you'll be stung. Can't stand your grizzling.

LESTER: What are you talking about?

ORIEL: Last time a cobbler stung you we had to load you onto the flatbed—

HAT: And I had to drive!—

ORIEL: And we delivered you to that doctor, naked and screaming like a breech birth.

> The KIDS *laugh.* LESTER *puts on his shoes.*

LESTER: All right, no stings tonight. Give us a kiss then. Quick, you wanna go, right?

QUICK: Yeah.

LESTER: Where's your brother?

QUICK: Dunno.

ORIEL: Fish? Fish?!

LESTER: Where are you, boy? Fish?

ORIEL: Fish?

QUICK: Fish?

> *Everyone calls up and down the riverbank.* FISH *appears out of darkness, swinging on a rope.*

FISH: Boo!

EVERYONE: [*overlapping*] Fish! / Don't do that! / Oh, Lord!

> FISH *leaps off the rope, lands and feigns breaking his leg. He hobbles towards* ORIEL, *who panics.*

ORIEL: Oh, Lord...

> FISH *hoots with laughter and straightens up.*

Samson Lamb!

> *All laugh at* FISH's *trick and* ORIEL's *fury.*

LESTER: Come on boys, let's get some tucker.

LON: Prawns! Prawns!

> ORIEL *darns on the beach;* HAT *cuddles* LON; RED *and* ELAINE *collect firewood.* QUICK, FISH *and* LESTER *walk into the water.* LESTER *holds a lantern. They spread the net.*

Don't grin so much, Fish, you'll frighten the prawns away. Come on, Quick, don't be so slow.

FISH: You're one to talk, Dad.

> *They have fanned out across the water. The* GIRLS *build a fire.* HAT *sings softly to* LON.

Oi, Quick, look at Dad. He looks like a statue in a fountain with that light. Wants to be careful someone don't toss a penny in and make a wish.

QUICK: What would they wish for, you reckon?
LESTER: Yeah, what?
FISH: Prolly wish they could get their money back.
LESTER: Cheeky blighter. Okay, start runnin' 'em towards me, boys.

They start the net towards their father.

RED: Ow! Ow! Ow!
ORIEL: What's the matter, love? You get stung?
RED: No! No! It's a crab! Oh, he's gone! Bugger!
ORIEL: Red!
RED: He bit me on the bum, Mum. What a perve!
LESTER: Where'd you learn such language?
RED: Elaine!

QUICK *speaks directly to the audience, as he and other characters will do from time to time throughout the play.*

QUICK: The water has never been so quiet. Quick, Fish and their father move through it like a cloud. Quick knows that everybody loves Fish. He's the handsome kid, the smart kid who makes people laugh. Even his three sisters, Hattie, Elaine and Red, love Fish, and they hate boys to hell and back.
ORIEL: Lest? Lester, where's Fish?
LESTER: Quick, where's your brother? He mucking around again?
QUICK: Fish?
LESTER: Fish! Come on, boy!
ORIEL: Fish?! Where are you?

QUICK *sees the shape in the water.*

QUICK: He's under it, he's under the net! Get it off!

All run into the water searching for FISH.

ORIEL: Do you see him?
QUICK: No, I lost him.
HAT: Where is he?
RED: Fish! Fish, are you joking? You better not be…
QUICK: Just pull! Pull!
LESTER: What?
QUICK: The net. Into the shallows. If he's caught in the net… Just pull it in!

3

HAT: Where is he, Quick?

All pull the net. LESTER *loses the lantern in the water.*

LESTER: Oh, the lamp! I don't see him!

RED: Fish!

ORIEL: Oh, Lord!

QUICK: There he is!

They see a shape in the net and run to it. LESTER *and* ORIEL *untangle* FISH.

LESTER: Oh, Lord.

No breath or movement from FISH. HAT *and* ELAINE *cry.*

RED: Is he dead?

ORIEL: No! No!

She beats on FISH*'s chest.*

Blessed Saviour, bring him back. Show us all Thy tender mercy and bring this boy back—

LESTER: Get the truck! We got to get him to hospital!

ORIEL: God, Jesus Almighty, raise him up! Now, you raise him up!

LESTER: Yes, Lord, yes!

There's still no sound or movement from FISH.

ORIEL: Lord Jesus!

She smashes FISH *on the chest one more time. Water spews from his mouth. He screams, but all cry with joy as he starts to breathe.*

LESTER: He's alive! He's alive!

ORIEL: It's a miracle! Praise the Lord of miracles!

LESTER *leads the* LAMBS *in singing: 'What a friend we have in Jesus...'*

QUICK: They drive Fish back into town. The Lambs barrel down the hill like mad bastards, singing and shouting. They swing into the dirt yard of the Church of Christ, ready to beat the door down, to find the minister, to tell the people: We got him back! Fish Lamb is back! Praise the Lord!

QUICK *cradles* FISH*'s head in his hands.*

4

But Quick holds his brother's head in his hands and knows it isn't quite right. Because not all of Fish Lamb has come back.

QUICK *looks towards the singing* LAMBS.

Dad? Mum? Look... Dad, Mum...

SCENE 2

SAM *screams as he catches his hand in the winch of the guano barge on which he works.*

SAM: Aaagh! Fuck!
QUICK: Dad? Mum?

ROSE *runs headlong through the space.*

ROSE: Mum! Mum!

She passes her brothers, CHUB *and* TED, *heading in the other direction. They don't listen to her.*

Ted? Chub? Wait. Dad's had an accident. It's his hand...
CHUB: Come on, we're goin' down the jetty!

She runs into a hotel towards her mother's room. DOLLY PICKLES *sits on the lap of a* PILOT, *fucking him well.*

ROSE: Mum...

DOLLY *puts her hand over the* PILOT's *mouth.*

Mum?

ROSE *retreats.* DOLLY *removes her hand from the* PILOT's *mouth. She licks his neck.*

PILOT: You're a damn good-looking woman, Mrs Pickles.
DOLLY: You Yanks are something. Jesus Christ, you're something. I like the salt when you sweat.

They keep fucking.

SCENE 3

Hospital, Geraldton. SAM, *his fist bandaged up in a salute, sits in a chair, groggy with pain killers.* ROSE *is with him.*

ROSE: Rose's dad, Sam Pickles, believes in luck, though he never says the word. He calls it the Shifty Shadow of God. And you never know which way it's going to fall. Rose has never felt the shadow the way she did today. She knew something bad was going to happen, something really bad, but she never thought the shadow would make her father lose his fingers working on a barge loaded with birdshit.

DOLLY, TED *and* CHUB *arrive.*

DOLLY: How is he?

ROSE: Four fingers and the top of his thumb.

DOLLY: The sister told me. His right hand?

ROSE: Yup. He caught it in the winch.

DOLLY: His bloody working hand. A man can hardly pick his nose with a thumb and half a pointer. Well, we're done, kids, we're cactus. Thank you, Lady Luck, you rotten slut. He been awake?

ROSE: No. I just been watching him. Wondering where you were.

TED: Can we go down to the jetty? If he's not gunna wake up…

ROSE: Supposed to be in school, youse.

TED: We'll be back dreckly. Dad might be awake then, eh, Mum?

ROSE: Don't drown from crying, Ted.

TED: You don't want to come 'cause last time you got a jellyfish up your bathers.

ROSE: No, 'cause someone thought you were my brother.

CHUB: But he is your brother.

TED: Right, Chub. Come on.

TED *runs off.*

CHUB: Know what I reckon? I reckon it'll be pretty good having a dad with bits off him. Everyone'll think he's a war hero.

DOLLY: Chub?

CHUB: Yeah?

DOLLY: Shut up and go to the jetty.

CHUB *runs off.* DOLLY *stares after him.*

A war hero? Wounded in the battle for birdshit? You can't get much mileage out of that.

DOLLY *goes.* ROSE *stays by* SAM.

ROSE: Rose watches Sam sleep. She hates him sometimes, he's so useless. She wants to hit him, to pick up a lump of four-by-two and snot him with it. He's a grown man and yet he doesn't have

6

a pinch of sense. But he isn't mean like the old girl. Rose knows something sour is coming into everything, and it's been happening all year. Everything is falling to bits.

SCENE 4

Margaret River. The LAMBS *pack the truck.*

RED: Do we have to go?

ORIEL: That's enough, Red.

ELAINE: Why are we leaving? Dad?

LESTER: Time we showed you all a bit of the world. All aboard.

ORIEL: Come on, Fish. Fish?

> FISH *doesn't respond.*

Quick, have you changed him?

QUICK: Yes, Mum. Come on, mate.

FISH: The water.

> FISH *gets in the truck.*

LESTER: When the Lambs roll down the main street, no-one even pauses in their business to wave. At the Margaret River bridge, someone mutters...

COUSIN FRED: There they go, poor silly Bible-bashing bastards.

LESTER: You can't stay in a town when everything blows up in your face, especially the only miracle that ever happened to you.

SCENE 5

Hospital. SAM's *hand is out of its bandage. He holds up a cigarette.*

SAM: I've learnt to roll a fag.

ROSE: Good on you, Dad.

SAM: Look what they gave me.

> *He holds up a small jar.* ROSE *presses her nose to it.*

ROSE: What is it?

SAM: It's my four fingers. And the nub of my thumb...

> ROSE *shudders, hands the jar to* DOLLY.

DOLLY: They look like half a pound of prawns.

7

SAM *laughs.*

ROSE: Doesn't matter, Dad. You're okay.

DOLLY: What are you going to do for a quid? Sam?

SAM: I'll go to work for cousin Joel. He'll give me a job. Joel's a lightning rod for luck. He bought that pub on his winnings from a horse called Eurhythmic. Did you know that? Now, that's luck. But I got my old man's blood. Dead unlucky.

ROSE: Until your luck changes, Dad.

SAM: Luck don't change, love. It moves.

> *Funeral bells. The* PICKLES FAMILY *assemble with their bags. A* LAWYER *reads a will.*

SCENE 6

LAWYER: 'I, Joel Morris Bloom...'

DOLLY: A heart attack at fifty. You call that lucky?

SAM: Well, he died haulin' in the biggest fish he ever caught.

LAWYER: '... direct that the Eurhythmic Hotel be sold, and the proceeds, together with the residue of my estate, be given to—'

SAM: My cousin Sam.

LAWYER: '... the Geraldton Turf Club, except for the sum of two thousand pounds, which I bequeath to my cousin Samuel Manifold Pickles...'

CHUB: Who's that?

ROSE: Shut up!

LAWYER: '... together with a property at Number One Cloud Street, Perth...'

TED: Perth!

SAM: Good old Joel! I knew he wouldn't forget me.

LAWYER: '... on condition that the said Samuel Manifold Pickles will not sell the said property for twenty years.'

DOLLY: Well, we're not movin' to Perth!

SAM: Nowhere else to go, Doll.

SCENE 7

Cloudstreet. The PICKLES FAMILY *approach the tumbledown old house.*

SAM: It's bloody huge!

DOLLY: Bloody strange, if you ask me.

SAM *leads them inside. They explore the house.*

TED: Where do we sleep tonight?

SAM: There's twenty rooms, son, take your pick.

CHUB: I'm hungry!

DOLLY: Suck your thumb.

TED: I hate it.

SAM: Go on, take a look around. Cloudstreet...

ROSE, TED *and* CHUB *go to explore.*

Got a good sound to it, don't you reckon? It's a bit run down, needs a paint, but your old man's had a win, love, a big win. The Shifty Shadow's shifted. Can't you feel it?

He's heading out.

DOLLY: Where are you going?

SAM: Nowhere.

DOLLY: Sam Pickles...

SAM: There's a horse running today called Silver Lining. That's got to be a sign, eh?

DOLLY: What are you bettin' with?

SAM: Have some faith, Doll.

DOLLY: Joel left that money to all of us.

SAM: Don't worry. I always come out even.

DOLLY: Sam! That horse'll be legless. Don't do it!

SAM: See you.

He's gone.

DOLLY: You bastard!

She chases after him. ROSE *finds the windowless room.*

ROSE: Hey, this room's got no windows...

SCENE 8

ROSE *explores the room, which is shadowed by ghosts of the house. She sees a piano.*

BLACK MAN: Once upon a time there was a big house owned by a respectable white woman who had cheated several people to get

9

it. But the local Anglican minister believed there is good in every heart, and it only needs to be nurtured. He put a proposition to her: 'Why not make your house a mission for young native women? Then all of Perth would remember you with gratitude.'

She filled her house with black girls. She aimed to make ladies out of them so they could set a standard for the rest of their sorry race. She showed them how to serve at table and how to wear hats in church, and she locked them in at night. The girls climbed into bed with one another and cried. They had been taken from their families and were not happy. They crawled out of windows but were tracked down and brought back.

One night one young girl went into the library, a room that had no windows. There she drank ant poison and died. The widow kicked out the rest of the girls and burned their linen under the fruit trees in the backyard.

A few weeks later she was at the piano when her heart stopped. Her nose hit Middle C. That's how the minister found the woman. Her smell knocked him over like a shot from a .303. The house was boarded up and it held its breath. Until today, no-one ever lived in it again, though some swore they could hear Middle C ringing from it at night.

ROSE *hits Middle C. She feels the presence of the ghosts and flees the room.*

SCENE 9

SAM *hangs a sign—ROOMS TO RENT—on the front of Cloudstreet.* DOLLY *watches, smoking.*

DOLLY: Two thousand quid down the dunny. More dough than we'd ever seen in our lives. We're poor again, dammit, shitpoor with a house as big as a church that we can't bloody sell.

SAM: I always come out even...

DOLLY: You're on a losing streak, Pickles, and it'll last as long as your life.

CHUB, TED *and* ROSE *come home from school.*

TED: Hey, the door of my room's locked!

DOLLY: 'Cause it's not your room anymore. You'll be in with Chub.

TED: Rather sleep with you, Ma.

> DOLLY *hoots, ruffles his hair.*

CHUB: They're all locked. All this side.

DOLLY: Your father's had an idea! He's renting out half the house. I'm going to be a friggin' landlady. Twenty years. I'm too young to be tied down like that. Twenty friggin' years.

TED: That's our friggin' luck. House and no money.

CHUB: Ponds and no fish.

TED: Trees and no fruit.

CHUB: Arm and no hand.

ROSE: Oh, you're a pair of real cards. Real funny blokes.

TED: I reckon this is a friggin' house of cards. And guess who's the bloody joker?

> DOLLY, TED *and* CHUB *go inside the house.* ROSE *finds her father dividing the house in two.*

ROSE: What's all this?

SAM: Bet you never thought you'd be a landlord's daughter, Rosebud.

ROSE: A person like you shouldn't even say the word bet.

SCENE 10

The LAMBS *arrive at Cloudstreet, perhaps in their old truck piled with furniture.* ORIEL *has a newspaper.*

LESTER: You sure this is it?

ORIEL: Last on the page. Number One Cloud Street. Go on, Lest. Go in and tee it up. The kids are exhausted. Tell them what we want.

> LESTER *heads towards the front door.*

QUICK: Looks flamin' haunted.

ORIEL: We'll be haunting it from now on. But don't worry. We're not here to stay, kids. This is just temporary. Till we get back on our feet.

> LESTER *knocks.* DOLLY *opens the door.*

DOLLY: Yeah? Sorry, mate, we're not buyin' nothin'. Try up the street a bit. You're as white as a ghost.

LESTER: It's limestone dust. We came up from the country. Margaret River.

DOLLY: Knew a bloke from there once. Had hair growin' out his nostrils.

LESTER: It's about the house…

DOLLY: Right. I'll get the hubby. Sam? Sam! Come down here, Sam. Stop buggerizin' about!

LESTER: My name's Lester Lamb.

SAM *appears.*

DOLLY: His name's Lester Lamb.

SAM *offers his left hand.*

SAM: Come and have a look. You get half the house, half the yard, your own dunny. The corridors are everyone's, same as the stairs. Bloody big joint, eh?

LESTER: I got six kids.

SAM: Catholics, eh?

LESTER: No. No, nothin'.

SAM: Can youse pay?

LESTER: We'll pay.

SAM: You'll do. [*He sees* ORIEL *with the* KIDS.] My name's Pickles. Sam Pickles. It's gunna sound like a counter lunch, Lamb and Pickles. Well, bring 'em in.

ROSE, CHUB *and* TED *watch* ORIEL *directing as the* LAMBS *unpack and move into their half of the house.*

ROSE: Cripes, and I thought *we* looked like reffos.

TED: Three girls. Whacko!

CHUB: There's three boys, too.

TED: One's a slowbo.

ROSE: Is not.

TED: Betcha.

SAM *joins them.*

Who are they?

SAM: They're called the Lambs.

TED: God, we're livin' with sheep!

SAM: This is their half now. They pay rent, so keep away. Time for youse to be in bed. You got school tomorrow.

CHUB: I'm not going to school.

SAM: Get to bed.

TED *and* CHUB *go.*

ROSE: You shouldn't have done this.

SAM: Shut up. I'm your father.

They see FISH LAMB *staring at them.*

FISH: Mister... who stoled your fingers?

QUICK *comes for him.*

QUICK: Come on, Fish. [*To* SAM] Sorry.

He leads FISH *away.* ROSE *stares at them.*

SAM: Who stoled your fingers? That's a good one, eh?

ROSE *goes.* SAM *surveys his stump.*

SCENE 11

Night. FISH *moves into the windowless room. He plays a note on the piano and the* GHOSTS *swirl above him.* FISH *can see them.*

FISH: G'day. I'm Fish. Fish Lamb. Who are you?

The GHOSTS *whisper in his ears.* FISH *reacts to the private story.*

No. Sad. Sad.

ROSE *appears in the doorway, unseen, and watches* FISH. *She doesn't see the* GHOSTS.

ROSE: I could read you stories.

The GHOSTS *leave* FISH.

I like reading. Do you like stories?

FISH: Where are the ladies?

ROSE: This room gives me the creeps.

QUICK *comes in and finds them.*

It's funny. Dad's divvied up all the rooms, but nobody gets this one. He calls it No Man's Land. Don't you reckon it smells? Or is it just that it's got no windows? Ted reckons you're a slowbo. I think you're beautiful.

She sees QUICK *and hurries away.*

QUICK: Hear that, Fish? She reckons you're beautiful. Come on, back to bed, mate.

13

FISH: See the lady?

QUICK *leads him away from the room.*

QUICK: That's just the girl from the other side.

FISH: No. The lady. Look.

QUICK *puts* FISH *to bed, then climbs in and goes to sleep.*
Can you hear it, Quick? The ladies are fighting. The house is sad. Can you hear it?

SCENE 12

LESTER *and* ORIEL *are by themselves.*

LESTER: Quick's looking blue.

ORIEL: Well, that's natural enough.

LESTER: Blames himself, thinks we blame him.

ORIEL: Don't we?

LESTER: It wasn't his fault. Why would it be?

ORIEL: But we blame him. And I blame you. And God.

LESTER: It scares me, hearing you talk like that.

ORIEL: Me too. I can't help it. I'm a sinner, Lest.

LESTER: What about Fish? What are we going to do with him?

ORIEL: We'll give him the gentlest life we can. We'll make it the best for him we know how.

LESTER: Orry? You think we should... take him to a doctor?

ORIEL: I'm not too chuffed about doctors, Lester. Neither are you.

LESTER: I know, but—

ORIEL: Hard work and plenty of food, that keeps the quacks away. And a bit of care. We'll do our best for Fish, and that's that.

LESTER: Please, Orry...

SCENE 13

Surgery. A DOCTOR *stares down* FISH's *throat with a light.* FISH *giggles.* ORIEL *sits with* QUICK. LESTER *puts his hands on* FISH's *shoulders as the* DOCTOR *examines him.*

DOCTOR: What's your name, boy?

ORIEL: Fish Lamb. Samson.

FISH: Fish.

DOCTOR: Mrs Lamb, I'll ask and he'll answer.

ORIEL: Very well.

DOCTOR: Why do they call you Fish?

FISH: It's the name.

LESTER: We called him Fish, 'cause of his wit, his alertness, Doctor.

DOCTOR: Hmm. How old are you, Fish?

FISH: Nine.

ORIEL: Ten next month.

DOCTOR: Mrs Lamb! [*To* FISH] Can you count to nine?

FISH: Nine.

DOCTOR: Yes.

FISH: I'm big.

DOCTOR: Indeed. Fish, where do you live?

FISH: In the family. With Quick, Lestah...

DOCTOR: Who is this?

FISH: Lestah! My da.

DOCTOR: And who is this, Fish? Who is this lady? Fish?

Silence.

ORIEL: Lester, he doesn't see me.

DOCTOR: Who is she, Fish?

LESTER: Please, Doctor, this—

FISH: The water.

DOCTOR: Queer. How long was he under the water?

LESTER: A few minutes. He was caught up under the net and my lamp went out—

DOCTOR: Yes. And you revived him, Mrs Lamb?

ORIEL: Yes. And I prayed.

FISH: The water.

DOCTOR: And you didn't take him to a doctor, or a hospital?

LESTER: We thought he was better. A miracle, you know.

DOCTOR: Hmm. Like Lazarus? Jesus wept.

ORIEL: But he's retarded. We had to potty train him again, start from scratch.

DOCTOR: You mean, he's improved?

LESTER: A bit, yes.

DOCTOR: A boy would have more than this regression after an experience like that.

15

ORIEL: Are you saying we're liars?

DOCTOR: Mrs Lamb—

ORIEL: I am a woman whose word has been respected as long—

LESTER: Oriel!—

DOCTOR: This boy seems traumatised. Are you sure he hasn't been through a great shock of some kind?

LESTER: He's been alive and he's been dead. One of those was bound to be a shock.

DOCTOR: You should think about a specialised home for him...

ORIEL: There's no home as specialised as mine, Mister!

> *She takes hold of* FISH.

FISH: Lestah! Lestah!

DOCTOR: Mrs Lamb, sit down.

ORIEL: Come on, Lester.

DOCTOR: Fish, where do you want to go?

FISH: The water, the water!

> ORIEL *bundles* FISH *out of the office.*

Fast! Fast!

SCENE 14

Cloudstreet kitchen. All the LAMBS *are there.* RED *spins the knife while* ELAINE *and* HAT *watch.*

HAT: This is for who washes up tonight!

RED: And this week! All this week!

ELAINE: The knife never lies, you know. It always knows best!

FISH: I wanna play! Come on, Lestah! Quick!

LESTER: It's slowing down! It's you, Hat.

HAT: Nah, got plenty in it yet. It's you, Dad.

LESTER: Nope. It's gonna be Quick. Look at him. He's getting out the tea-towel already, aren't you, mate? Here it comes again.

RED: Elaine!

ELAINE: Wait. Wait!

QUICK: Oh, God!

HAT / ELAINE / RED: Quick! Quick gets the dishes.

LESTER: The knife never tells a fib, but it can make a bib for a squib. Here's one. Who's got a pimple up their dimple?

16

Laughter as he spins the knife again.

Who will it be? Round and round and round it goes, and where it stops...

RED: It's... it's Elaine. Pimple up your dimple, Ee!

ELAINE: It's not!

HAT: Carn, Ee, fair cop!

QUICK: Yeah, the knife doesn't lie!

LESTER: You kids wash up. I'll just be a tick.

The KIDS *go.*

We're making something here, love, I can feel it.

ORIEL: We need things.

LESTER: Plenty.

ORIEL: Don't smile me down, Lest.

LESTER: There's money left, love. We're not hungry.

ORIEL: We need work.

LESTER: I've been thinking some more.

ORIEL: Thought I smelt burning rubber.

LESTER: Thinking about this place.

ORIEL: Don't bother. It's time we were moving on. We need our own bathroom. We need a stove, the kids need clothes. They go to school like they haven't got a mother. This place is only temporary. We need to find somewhere permanent.

LESTER: Hang on. I've cottoned onto something. There's no corner shop this side of the railway line.

ORIEL: I know. I've carried the groceries back from Subi.

LESTER: I've brained it out. We could do it.

ORIEL: What are you talking about?

LESTER: A shop. Our shop.

ORIEL: Is this another one of your—?

LESTER: This is a good one, Orry.

ORIEL: Don't be a fool, Lest. We can't pay rent on a shop.

LESTER: We already are. Right now.

ORIEL: What've you done?

LESTER: I've used my noggin.

ORIEL: Explain.

LESTER: We'll use that front room for a shop.

ORIEL: Across the corridor, they'll chuck all whatsername about it.

LESTER: They're broke, darl. They're poor as us. And lazy. Look at them, waiting for the boat to come in. They need the money. We'll pray about it. We'll take it to the Lord. No, wait on... [*He spins the knife.*] The knife never lies. If it points to me it's a Yes. To you, it's a No.

> *They watch the knife spin. It points to* LESTER.

ORIEL: How do you know it never lies?

> LESTER *looks towards the* MUSICIAN *who watches the scene.*

LESTER: What'll it be?

ORIEL: Somethin' I don't know. Play me somethin' I don't know.

> LESTER *breaks into a song.*

SCENE 15

The LAMBS *set the shop up.* LESTER *hangs out a sign: LAMBS' MIXED BUSINESS: WE'RE LOCAL, WE'RE HONEST, WE'RE HERE. GERRY CLAY passes in uniform, notices DOLLY. She sees the sign.*

DOLLY: 'We're local, we're honest, we're here.' Wouldn't it turn your guts? [*To* ORIEL] Well, how's it doing, ducks?

ORIEL: Bit of a slow start. But we'll be right. If there's one thing we've got, it's stickability.

DOLLY: Stickability. How much you made so far?

LESTER: A shilling and a ha'penny.

DOLLY: Oh, you'll get rich if you keep this up.

ORIEL: And you'll have an income, Mrs Pickles. Is there anything I can get you?

DOLLY: Oh. Couple of spuds?

> LESTER *gives the* KIDS *a lolly.* ORIEL *bags the spuds.*

ORIEL: There. That'll be—

LESTER: On the house.

> DOLLY *takes the potatoes. She sees a row of cakes.*

ELAINE: Dad baked these.

DOLLY: Good for him.

> DOLLY *leaves. A scream from behind the shop.* HAT *emerges.*

HAT: That Ted Pickles showed me his thing!

RED *picks up a pair of scissors.*

RED: Right let's get him.

She leads the LAMB GIRLS *off.* DOLLY *laughs, beckons to* TED *as* ROSE *and* CHUB *come home from school.*

DOLLY: There's my boy. Got a kiss for your old mum?

She embraces TED.

CHUB: Mum, Hitler shot himself in his bunk.

TED: Bunker, Chub. Does that mean the war's over?

DOLLY: They still got to clean up the Nips, Teddy.

TED: Oh, yeah...

CHUB: What's for tea, Mum?

DOLLY: Christ knows.

SAM *comes home, sees the shop sign.*

SAM: What do you reckon? We're local, we're honest, we're bloody mad.

DOLLY: Least they're earning a quid. More than I can say for anyone on our side of the house. It's like this place has had a stroke, Sam. Paralysed down one side.

She gives ROSE *the potatoes and goes.*

ROSE: I'll get the tea on.

SAM: That's the girl.

SCENE 16

QUICK *reads a newspaper in his room.*

QUICK: Quick Lamb reads the paper every day and sees the long lists of the missing believed killed, and the notices in memoriam for sons and fathers and brothers. The war's over, he knows, but he picks up sadness like he's got radar for it. The whole world's trying to get back to peace, but somewhere there's craters and rubble and gas chambers, and still the stories coming home as though it'll never let itself be over. 'We're lucky,' he thinks. 'The old man was too old and I was too young. We've got food, coupons, a full ration book. We're gettin' away light.'

ORIEL *gives him food. He goes to the schoolyard.*

Quick sees kids at school who are poor. Through the winter, Quick notices Wogga McBride. He has a queer way of eating his sandwich, hiding it under his hand. Maybe it's Quick's misery radar, but he can't let it be, till eventually he sees that Wogga hasn't got a sandwich at all.

He watches WOGGA McBRIDE *pretending to eat.*

The Lambs are patched and barefooted, but at lunchtime their mother always brings warm pies and pasties from the shop.

He takes food to WOGGA.

I'm full. Want this?

WOGGA *runs away.* QUICK *watches him go.*

Wogga lives further down the tracks towards West Perth, but he crosses at the walkway below Cloudstreet. Today is the last day of primary school, and if Quick doesn't make friends with him today, he never will. He tails him down Rokeby Road, past the football ground and up the embankment behind West Leederville station. Down beside the tracks Wogga's fooling with a stray dog that's got hold of his school bag. Quick hears Wogga laughing, even over the sound of an approaching train. Quick wants to go down and run the dog ragged with him. And then Wogga tears the bag free of the dog and sways back, shrieking with glee, and the sleeper catches his heel and he staggers and the engine smacks him with the sound of a watermelon falling off the back of a truck, and he's gone.

Noise and light. WOGGA *disappears.* QUICK *runs.*

SCENE 17

Cloudstreet. QUICK *runs headlong into his room. He finds a large stack of old newspapers. He starts to cry.* FISH *comes in.*

FISH: What you laughing for, Quick?

QUICK *stops crying, ignores* FISH.

QUICK: Off you go, mate.
FISH: Off you go, mate. You happy, Quick?
QUICK: Go away, Fish.
FISH: You sad?

20

QUICK: Mate, everybody gets sad. You get sad.

FISH: When I want the water.

QUICK: What water?

FISH: The water, the water.

LESTER *sees them together.*

QUICK: Fish, go and play with Lon, mate. Or the girls. Go on.

FISH *goes.* QUICK *is alone with the stack of old newspapers. He starts searching through them.* LESTER *watches.*

Quick doesn't let himself think about what happened to Wogga. Quick thinks about nothing at all. He just hears the scissors going as he cuts out pictures, hears himself thumbing tacks into his wall. And the people in all the pictures, the burnt babies, the amputee diggers, the walking dead, they laugh at Quick, all of them, and they dance with Wogga McBride along the tracks.

LESTER: A lot of sad people, Quick. What are you doin' with them?

QUICK *cuts, or puts the pictures up.*

Knocks me round to see you like this, boy. Three days we haven't seen you downstairs. You'll starve to death. Look at these poor sods. You don't want to be like them. You don't need to be. You've got a roof over your head, family... well, we're not much, but strike... Look, come downstairs. For your mother's sake.

QUICK *goes on cutting.*

Well, do it for Fish. Come on. He's worried sick about you.

QUICK *goes on cutting.*

You know damn well your brother is busted in the head and he'll never grow up right. The least you can do is let him be happy. Don't torture him, Quick. And us. You're feeling sorry for yourself and it's making me sick. You and me understand about Fish. We were there, we were stupid enough to drown him trying to save him. You remember that. We owe him things, Quick. All we can do now is let him be happy. I can sit here and talk and get nothing back for as long as it takes to get angry enough to swat your arse and send your mother up to deal with you. But Fish, he'll wait. He'll wait till you say something to him. Don't you

21

forget about Fish, boy. Not as long as you live, or your life won't have been worth living.

Silence. LESTER *leaves* QUICK *alone. He goes on cutting.*

SCENE 18

PICKLES *side of the house.* ROSE *comes home from school with* TED *and* CHUB, *who carries two schoolbags.*

CHUB: Carn, Ted, I'm tired...

TED: Don't be a whacker! Carry it!

They are gone. ROSE *sees* SAM *coming home.*

ROSE: Where have you been?

SAM: Come here, Rosie.

ROSE: You've been gone two days. I thought I was going to have to tough it out with Mum for the rest of my life.

SAM: I got a job.

ROSE: A job! How?

SAM: The shifty shadow, Rosie.

She snorts.

True as my word.

ROSE: How?

SAM *rattles pennies.*

Two-up? You've got to be joking, Dad.

SAM: I put a bloke so far in the red he had to pay in kind. He's a union boss. He owes me a job. Start Monday. I'll be makin' millions, Rosie.

ROSE: Don't get beyond yourself.

SAM: No, fair dinkum. It's a job at the Mint.

ROSE: The Mint? I hope they don't find out you count on your fingers.

SAM: Cheeky bugger!

DOLLY *comes out of the house.*

DOLLY: About bloody time.

ROSE: She was worried sick, I don't think.

ROSE *goes inside.*

SAM: Got myself a job, Doll. Old Sam's back on the boil. I'm
cashed up. What say we go out and celebrate tonight?

He tries to embrace her. She resists.

DOLLY: I've made other plans.

SAM: You off somewhere? Mind if I tag along?

DOLLY: Yes, I do. I told you, I've got other plans.

She hurries away.

SCENE 19

SAM: Sam tries to help Rose around the house. But he's not much
good with one hand. Sam tries to keep out of Dolly's way but
ends up botherin' her more than ever. And Sam tries not to blow
all the money he's making at the Mint. But he starts backing a
horse named Blackbutt. And, believe it or not, that son-of-a-gun
just won't lose, not for three months.

SAM *watches* LESTER *in the backyard.*

G'day. You look knackered. Me too. Still gettin' used to regular
work.

LESTER: Ah. Know how you feel.

SAM: I ache down one side now, you know, 'cause of this. See. I
favour the other arm. Makes it hurt like buggery.

LESTER: They say you feel the pain, even when there's nothin'
there.

SAM: More an itch you get now and then, if you catch my drift, and
a man goes to scratch it and there's nothin' to scratch.

LESTER: How did you... How did it...?

SAM: A winch. On a boat. Just bloody stupidity. And bad luck, Mr
Lamb. You believe in luck, Mr Lamb?

LESTER: Call me Lest.

SAM: All right, Lest. Call me Sam. Or landlord'll do, if you're stuck
for words. I've been on wharves and boats all my life. Now I'm
at the Mint. Sort of like a utility man, push a broom, take turns
lookin' for duds. Not a lot a fella with one hand can do. You
know they just cook money? Like my old lady cooks a batch of
scones. Except more regular. And a bit softer. Out they come,
pennies, zacks, deeners, shillings. The place stinks of it. You feel

23

it in your hair and on your clobber. Spend all day breathin' in gold dust. The place is like a cake shop and the smell always gets you hungry. You believe in luck, Lest?

LESTER: Can't say.

SAM: I'm on a run.

LESTER: How do you mean?

SAM: Like I'm winnin'. Luck, it's like a light shinin' on you. You can feel it. I'll show you, if you like.

LESTER: How?

SAM: Horse I been bettin' on, called Blackbutt. Never lets me down. You can come with me today...

LESTER: I've only been to a racecourse once.

SAM: Once!

LESTER: Down Margaret. There was a revival meeting. I took Oriel and the kids. This bloke told the gospel story like an angel...

SAM: At a racecourse?

LESTER: I've never really been a bettin' man.

SAM: You won't be bettin', old son, you'll be investin' in success, you'll be baskin' in the glory. Revival meeting... Well, you must know that sayin' about gettin' tenfold of what you give. That's what we're gunna slip into today, cobber, you and me.

SCENE 20

ROSE *seeks* DOLLY *in a local pub.*

ROSE: Rose pushes through the sour stinking boozers in the public bar who shout through their noses and make wings of their elbows and holes of their mouths...

She is surrounded and oppressed by a crowd of BLOKES.

MALE VOICES: Not a touch on her old girl...
Come back in five years...
Come here, kid, I'm not fussy...
Skinny as a rake...
She's not Dolly's girl! Bullshit...

ROSE: Rose can't stay in here. She finds the door and shoves against it, and escapes into the clean night air. The noise and smoke of the pub stay inside.

DOLLY, *drunk, carries on with the* WOMEN *in the Ladies'
Lounge.* ROSE *hears, sees.*

Damn Dolly, damn her, damn her to hell and shit and piss and
sick! She's drunk again and loud and vile with her eyes full of
hate and meanness, but Rose'll get her out in the end. Rose'll
drag her home. Rose'll kick her shins, bite her arse. She'll get
her out.

ROSE *re-enters the pub, pushing through the* BLOKES *to find*
DOLLY.

Come home, Mum. God, you've been down here since this
morning.

DOLLY: Was it only this morning?

She makes the CROWD *laugh.*

ROSE: Mum, please. No-one's home. Not even Chub.

DOLLY: He'll come in when he's hungry.

ROSE: And who's going to feed him? Mum, you should be home.
Someone should be home.

DOLLY: Where's your father?

ROSE: He went to the races. I'm on my own.

DOLLY: You got all them Lambs next door.

SALLY: You got lambs next door, Doll?

DOLLY: The Lamb family. Them with the shop. Our tenants.

SALLY: I thought youse were the—

DOLLY: They're our tenants. It's our friggin' house, Sal.

ROSE: Please, Mum.

DOLLY: I'm busy. Go and do your homework.

ROSE: I've done it.

DOLLY: Well, read one of them books you lugged down from
Geraldton. She's a big reader, this one.

MAN: You got no boys running after you, Rose?

DOLLY: They were all over me when I was her age. But Rose'll be
safe. She's nothin' but skin and bone.

ROSE: Stop it.

DOLLY: Christ, you look like a bloody skeleton. People think we
starve you. Go home and feed yourself.

ROSE: Shouldn't that be your job?

GERRY CLAY *appears from the group of men.*

GERRY: You heard your mum. Go on, go home.

ROSE: So she can carry on all night with you drunken bludgers? She can do her drinking at home. She's got bottles stashed away in every room of the house...

DOLLY *slaps her.*

DOLLY: Don't you ever come after me again. Never!

ROSE: All right. I won't. Never!

ROSE *runs out of the pub.* GERRY *sidles up to* DOLLY.

GERRY: You sure she's yours?

DOLLY: Yeah.

GERRY: And who are you when you're not at home?

DOLLY: Who do you think I am?

GERRY: Well, you sound a bit like that Lauren Bacall.

DOLLY: You're a charmer. I sound like an old mother, a spud-peeler with a fag on her tongue.

GERRY: No, you don't.

DOLLY: Yes, I do.

GERRY: I've seen you around. You're no spud-peeler.

DOLLY: You been watching me?

GERRY: Yeah.

DOLLY: I seen you too. In your uniform. When you first got back.

GERRY: How'd I look?

DOLLY: The way a bloke should look.

GERRY: And how's that?

DOLLY *laughs. He leads her out of the hotel.*

Come on...

SCENE 21

Street outside the house. SAM *and* LESTER *roll home drunk from the races.*

LESTER: Good old Blackbutt!

SAM: Wasn't Blackbutt did it for us, Lest. It was the Shifty Shadow.

LESTER: You think we've drunk too much?

SAM: You still standin'?

LESTER: I think so. Those big boats down there are my shoes, unless I'm wrong, and I'm higher than them, so... [*He lurches, falls.*] Will I chuck up now?

SAM: If you feel it's important, Les, I suppose you'll get around to it.

LESTER: Never drunk liquor before, really.

SAM: And you're feelin' chunderish?

LESTER: No. Well... maybe.

> *He vomits.* SAM *pats him on the back.*

SAM: You okay, mate?

LESTER: Never better. We best... Shhh.

SAM: Yeah, shhhhh. 'Night.

LESTER: 'Night.

SAM: Good old Blackbutt, eh?

LESTER: Yeah, Good old Buttblack.

SCENE 22

LESTER *and* SAM *go quietly indoors.* QUICK *and* ROSE *are in their rooms.* QUICK *cuts out pictures.* ROSE *reads. When she hears* SAM *she tucks the book under her arm and goes to bring him his dinner.*

SAM: Where's the old girl?

> ROSE *shrugs.*

Looks a bit dry, Rosie.

ROSE: Too bad.

> *He tucks into his food.*

SAM: Good, but. You're getting very thin, Rose. Are you feeding yourself?

> *She nods.*

You sure? What's that you're reading?

ROSE: *Jane Eyre.*

SAM: Good? Few laughs in it? I could do with a laugh.

ROSE/ORIEL: How much did you lose?

SAM: I won, Rose. Never gonna lose again.

27

SCENE 23

LESTER *creeps in.* ORIEL *catches him.*

ORIEL: How much?
LESTER: A hundred and six quid.
SAM: The old Shifty Shadow's falling my way.
ORIEL: What about him?
LESTER: Sam?
ORIEL: So it's 'Sam' now? Come to bed, I don't want to know.
LESTER: In a tick.

> LESTER *goes to* QUICK'*s room.*

You should be asleep, son.
QUICK: Okay.

> QUICK *puts the scissors down.* LESTER *hugs* QUICK *who tries to pull away.*

Dad...
LESTER: I love you, Quick. You okay?
QUICK: I'm fine.

> LESTER *stares at the clippings.*

LESTER: I... worry about you.
QUICK: I'm fine.
LESTER: I won a lot of money today, son. What say we go to Fremantle tomorrow? Whole family! We'll drop a line from the wharf, get sunburnt, we'll let the harbour know we're there! Carn, we'll absolutely Lamb the place! How's that sound?
QUICK: Sounds good, Dad.
LESTER: That's what we'll do then. 'Night, son. I...

> LESTER *goes.*

SCENE 24

A rooster crows. DOLLY *comes home drunk and dishevelled, carrying her shoes.* TED *comes out of the house.*

DOLLY: Teddy...
TED: Where you been, Mum?
DOLLY: Come here, love. Give us a cuddle.

She pulls TED *close.*

You're growin' up fast. I seen the girls lookin' at you. You're killin' 'em, son. I can see it. They make me jealous, sometimes.

TED: Yeah?

DOLLY: You remind me of your dad, Teddy. But harder. A bit more steel. A bit less understanding. Oh, yeah, you're killin' 'em. I can see it, son.

SCENE 25

The LAMBS *are at the Fremantle wharf.* ORIEL *fishes.* HAT *counts the fish in her bucket.* FISH *stares at the water.* QUICK *sits near, watchful.* LON, RED *and* ELAINE *play on the beach.* LESTER *is nowhere to be seen.*

ORIEL: How many we got?

HAT: Ten if you count the flathead with one eye.

ORIEL: That'll do. Fish have gone off the bite anyway.

> LON *slams his foot down on something: bang!* RED *and* ELAINE *scream.*

ELAINE: Mum! Make him stop!

ORIEL: Lon, cut it out. Red, you seen your father?

RED: He's talking to some man down there.

> LON *stomps again: bang!*

ELAINE: Mum!

ORIEL: Lon, come here.

> *He runs up to her.*

What are you doing?

LON: You let the blowfish swell up all big and spiky, then you stomp on it, and bang!

ELAINE: There's guts and... oh, God...

ORIEL: You enjoyin' yourself? Like stomping on them fish?

LON: Yeah.

> *She clips him on the ear.*

ORIEL: Well stop it. Your sisters don't like it.

29

As the GIRLS *laugh,* LESTER *appears.* ORIEL *stares beyond him, seeing something.*

What's that?

LESTER: A boat. I bought it. Just walked up and offered the bloke money.

All stare at LESTER *except* FISH, *who watches the water.*

ORIEL: You'll never fit it on the back of the truck.

LESTER: Oh... No.

HAT: You'll have to row it home, Dad.

LESTER: How about you do it, son?

QUICK: On my own?

LESTER: You can take someone.

QUICK: Up river, you mean? All the way to Perth?

LESTER: Too right. You can do it.

ORIEL *storms into the truck and slams the door.*

You could put in at Crawley. That's not far from home.

HAT: It's miles, Dad. Don't be daft.

QUICK: I can do it.

LESTER: Right. Good bloke, Quick. Who's goin' with him as first mate?

QUICK: Fish. I want Fish.

Silence.

LESTER: All right. If he wants to. If you're careful.

QUICK *and* FISH *push off. All but* ORIEL *wave goodbye.*

SCENE 26

LESTER *and* ORIEL *in the kitchen at Cloudstreet.*

ORIEL: Has my life been a waste? Has it been that useless?

LESTER: What? What have I done?

ORIEL: They don't have a light. They could be anywhere. Can't you think? Can't you flamin' well, damn well, think, Lester, before you do such stupid, stupid—They're boys! They're just boys! You think you'd learn about rivers. You'd swear a man would get smart! You're not fit to have children!

ORIEL *goes.* LESTER *stares after her. Then he runs off.*

30

SCENE 27

FISH *and* QUICK *start their journey.* QUICK *keeps rowing.* FISH *loves it all.*

QUICK: All right?

FISH: The river's big.

QUICK: My oath. I'm nearly pooping myself.

> FISH *laughs.* QUICK *rows on.*

Cracker boat, eh?

FISH: Yeah.

QUICK: It's ours, Fish.

FISH: Whacko!

> QUICK *continues to row. The* BLACK MAN *watches them.*

BLACK MAN: It doesn't feel so bad to have sore hands when you know that you've left Fremantle behind and passed Rocky Bay with all its puking foundries and limestone cliffs, for the long stretch through Melville and the sugar factory. But Quick starts to wonder if the old man is the full quid. He's not sure if even a full-grown man could do this trip.

FISH: It's a long way. Is it a long way, Quick?

QUICK: Yeah, mate, it's a fair whack, orright.

FISH: Can I do?

QUICK: Do what?

FISH: Do the sticks. The rowers.

QUICK: All right, we'll share. Then we'll go faster, eh?

> FISH *climbs towards the oars. The boat totters.*

Don't roll us, Fish! Don't roll us.

> FISH *starts to row with* QUICK.

BLACK MAN: It's lucky they're headed in the long-bellied arc around the Mosman spit because that's the only direction they're likely to go in, the way Fish is rowing. Quick hopes Fish will get bored by the time they need a straight run, though he figures it'll be dark by then anyway.

> FISH, *tired of rowing, curls up at* QUICK*'s feet.*

Out past Claremont, out past somewhere, Quick doesn't know anymore, he stops. He sits back and ships the oars and gives it away.

31

QUICK: Well. What you thinkin'?

FISH: I can hear the water.

QUICK: We're on the water, you dill.

FISH: I can hear it.

QUICK: Yeah. You cold?

FISH: No.

QUICK: I'm knackered.

> FISH *stands and spreads his arms wide. The boat flies through the sky.*

BLACK MAN: Fish laughs like he's just found a mullet in his shorts and stands with his arms out like he's a bird sitting in an updraught. The sky, packed with stars, rests just above his head, and when Quick looks over the side he sees the river is full of sky as well. There's stars and swirl and space down there, and it's not water anymore. It doesn't even feel wet. There's no lights ashore now. There's no shore at all. Quick knows all the planets from school but he can't tell one from the other as they blur past. The boat's vibrating and the anchor's rattling and Fish tilts his wings in the bow. Quick could swear Fish is steering them. He feels fatigue coming to claim him and he strains to stay awake, to see, to see.

QUICK: Are we in the sky, Fish?

FISH: Yes, it's the water.

QUICK: What do you mean?

FISH: The water. The water. I fly.

SCENE 28

LESTER *runs along the shore, searching the river.*

LESTER: Quick! Quick! Fish! Quick! Lord, what a fool I am. You're right, Oriel! I'm not fit to have kids. Quick!

> LESTER *weeps.*

SCENE 29

QUICK *and* FISH *float in the boat. The magic has passed.*

FISH: The water!

QUICK: The river, Fish. We're back on the river.

FISH: Where's the water go?

QUICK: We're on it, mate.

FISH: No, it go!

BLACK MAN: Fish begins to whimper. Quick holds him. Like a baby, he thinks, and he's as big as me. All the excitement has disappeared. Quick knows the old misery again, but doesn't let himself break as he gives in to sleep.

SCENE 30

Riverbank. Dawn. LESTER *is exhausted.*

LESTER: Quick! Fish!

> *He finds the boat. His sons are there asleep. He lets out a whoop of joy and dances a jig.*

I found 'em! I found 'em, Orry!

QUICK: You all right, Dad?

> LESTER *dances as the boys paddle for shore.*

LESTER: I'm a blinking, useless idiot, son. I'm sorry.

QUICK: No, Dad. I'm glad I went.

LESTER: Are you? Do you feel better?

QUICK: Yeah. Yeah.

LESTER: Good.

SCENE 31

House, morning. LESTER, FISH *and* QUICK *return.* LESTER *sings...*

LESTER: This old man, he played one...

> ROSE, TED *and* CHUB *watch them from the house.* ORIEL *comes out from the shop to confront them.*

Truck ran out of juice, love. No juice and no money.

> ORIEL *hugs her boys.*

ORIEL: No brains, Lester Lamb. And no wonder.

> *She sees* QUICK's *blistered hands.*

Look at your hands.

QUICK: They're okay, Mum.

He goes to his room.

FISH: I'm hungry. Lestah, I'm hungry.

ORIEL: Who am I? Fish? I'm your mother.

FISH *pushes past* ORIEL *as though unable to see her.*

SCENE 32

FISH *finds* QUICK *in his room with the pictures.*

FISH: We flied, Quick. We flied!

QUICK: No, we didn't.

FISH: Yes. We goed in the stars.

QUICK: No.

QUICK *moves away and starts to cut out more pictures.* ROSE *reads.* QUICK *cuts.*

SCENE 33

DOLLY *is alone by the train tracks.*

DOLLY: Dolly follows the rails most nights, remembers those hot, buckling rails up there where childhood lived, remembers riding the rails with her father, remembers her sisters, and the big sister that hated her, remembers the poison in her heart. Here the moon lights up the steel so it looks deadly cool, and now and then she gets the feeling that she could just lie down there and go to sleep and the whole world, the whole fucking mess would evaporate. It's all too complicated, unless Dolly's as full as a goog, then it's simple, then all of it's straight in a girl's mind. And if she is full, some nights she doesn't walk the tracks alone.

GERRY CLAY *approaches.*

Of all the men she's met since Sam dragged her down from Geraldton, the one that sticks is Gerry Clay. There's something exciting about him. He's got muscle on him, and besides, he's a Catholic, and dead scared of going to Hell.

GERRY: You're a bottler, Doll. Bet your old man's a millionaire, the way you look.

DOLLY: Him? He hasn't got a pot to piss in. Give us a kiss, love.

GERRY: He give you a good knock, now and then?

DOLLY: If he did, I wouldn't be here. You've got a foul mouth, sport.

She kisses him.

SCENE 34

ORIEL: No one takes much notice of Mr and Mrs Clay when they open their shop on the main road. But walking past one day, Oriel sees the rival business with its big gaudy sign. 'G.M. Clay. Ex 2nd AIF. Buy here.' Buy here? Because he served his country in wartime? That's dirty...

ORIEL *visits the* CLAYS' *shop.*

GERRY: G'day, madam. What can I get you?

ORIEL: Oh. A dozen eggs, please.

GERRY: Righto.

He serves her.

That'll be sixpence ha'penny, thanks. Anything else?

ORIEL: No thank you. Mr Clay, where did you serve? The sign outside your shop says 'G. Clay. Ex 2nd AIF. Buy Here'.

GERRY: You'd be Mrs Lamb.

ORIEL: Where did you fight?

MRS CLAY: What's it to you, Mrs Lamb?

ORIEL: Well, if you're going to use it for advertising...

MRS CLAY: He was in New Guinea. On the Kokoda Trail.

ORIEL: Infantry?

GERRY: Signalman and runner, Mrs Lamb.

ORIEL: Oh. Fair enough.

She's going. MRS CLAY *stops her.*

MRS CLAY: Did your husband serve, Mrs Lamb?

ORIEL: Not this time. In the First World War. The 10th Light Horse. He was at Gallipoli. But we'd never skite about that.

MRS CLAY: What was his rank?

ORIEL: Well... private. He was a cook.

MRS CLAY *giggles.*

MRS CLAY: A cook? Well, you wouldn't skite about that, would you?

ORIEL *returns to Cloudstreet.*

ORIEL: If they want war, they've got war.

LESTER: We're doing all right, Orry. There's room for both shops.

ORIEL: Your cakes, Lester. That's our secret weapon. Cakes and pies and—oh, my Lord, I never thought of it! Summer's coming on...

SCENE 35

HAT, RED, ELAINE, LON *and* FISH *spruik.* FISH *rings a bell.* CHUB *watches, until he scores an ice cream.*

HAT: Get it quick! Get it now! While you're hot!

ELAINE: And while it's cold!

LON: Lester Lamb's Amazing Vanilla Double Cream Ice Cream!

RED: Only at Cloudstreet!

FISH: I scream! You scream! We all scream for ice cream!

RED: Every gallon means a discount on your smallgoods...

HAT: Fruit and vegies...

ELAINE: Pies and cakes...

RED: Get your Lester Lamb Amazing Vanilla Double Cream Ice Cream!

HAT: Rich creamy goodness...

ELAINE: Melts in your mouth...

RED: Runs out your bum...

CHUB, LON *and* FISH *guffaw.*

HAT / ELAINE: Red!

RED: Well, it does.

FISH: Runs out your bum...

ELAINE: Now look what you've started, Red Lamb!

CHUB: Milk, milk, lemonade, round the corner chocolate's made...

RED: Were we talking to you?

HAT: Shut up. Ring the bell, Fish.

FISH: Runs out your bum.

HAT *grabs the bell, rings it.*

HAT: Get it quick, get it now! Carn, I'm not doing this on my own.

ELAINE / RED: Get your Lester Lamb Amazing Vanilla Double Cream Ice Cream!

They hand free samples to some of the audience and finish their spruiking with a song.

SCENE 36

Street. MRS CLAY *intercepts* SAM *on his way home.*

MRS CLAY: Mr Pickles? Are you Sam Pickles?

SAM: Yeah, that's me.

MRS CLAY: You don't know me and I really don't know you, and I've got nothing against you or anything, but I think you should try to control your wife.

SAM: And I think you should mind your own bloody business, lady.

MRS CLAY: It is my business! It's my marriage I'm talking about. I've got young'uns to look after and she's got no right. If you were any kind of a man, you'd put a stop to it. It's a mortal sin!

MRS CLAY storms off. SAM raises his stump to the sky.

SAM: What am I going to do? Stump the bastard to death?

SCENE 37

SAM *finds* ROSE *dishing up in the kitchen.*

SAM: Sit down and eat something yourself. Jesus, Rose, you look like a corpse these days. It's a crime you know, a bloody crime.

ROSE: I get fat.

SAM: You haven't been fat since you were hangin' off a tit. Now you've grown your own. You have to start eatin' again. It's not a joke anymore, love.

ROSE: I can't, Dad. I just toss it back up again.

SAM: Bullshit. You've just talked yourself off your tucker. Go on, do it, bugger you!

He pushes his dinner in front of her.

I didn't go through a fuckin' depression and a world war to see my kid starve to death in my own house. Eat, Rose, eat.

She starts to eat. He goes. She spits out the food.

SCENE 38

Bathroom. SAM *finds his razor, opens it.* ROSE *finds him, sees the razor.*

ROSE: You need lather, Dad.
SAM: What are we gonna do, what are we all gonna do?

> ROSE *holds him. He sobs.*

ROSE: I don't know. You can't do it to me. I'd piss on your grave, I tell you I would.
SAM: Oh, you're a hard bastard. Do you hate me?
ROSE: No. I pity you. Because you still love her.
SAM: Rose, people are... who they are.
ROSE: Then they should change!
SAM: You'll go a long way.

> ROSE *is on her own.*

ROSE: Yes. Africa. Paris. New York. A long way from this stinking old house and the smell of death. I'll go like a shot one day.

SCENE 39

CHUB *is eating some of* LESTER*'s ice cream.*

CHUB: By the middle of summer, Lester Lamb's Amazing Vanilla is all the go. People buy the stuff before it has time to set. Every night the Lamb kids turn the churns, skim and sluice and measure and pour, and every day the ice cream walks out the door. The Subiaco Junior Cricket team forfeits a big match one Saturday morning because they've all gone for some of Lester's ice cream. Local ladies walk right past G.M. Clay ex-AIF, and join the queues at Cloudstreet. They pay in advance, they faint on the verandah, they plead for an extra serve of Vanilla Double Cream.

> ORIEL *and* LESTER *close up shop.*

ORIEL: Been a good day. Another good day.
ELAINE: I've got a dreadful headache.
LESTER: A woman today spent four quid on ice cream. Half a week's wages. Don't you reckon we might be going a bit far?

ORIEL: We didn't start this, Lester.

CHUB *passes.*

CHUB: Clays have closed up shop.

ORIEL: You're pulling my leg.

CHUB: Go round and look for yourself.

LESTER: Closed up? For good?

CHUB: Looks like it.

CHUB *goes.*

LESTER: Crikey. Clay's got kiddies, hasn't he? A squadron of them.

ORIEL: I'll go round there, Lester. If he'll just take the nonsense off the front of his shop...

She finds DOLLY *passing, bloodied and dishevelled.*

Mrs Pickles. What happened?

DOLLY: Parting gift from Gerry Clay. Spare me the blushes, Mrs Lamb. You did him, and he did me.

ORIEL: He never.

DOLLY: How much do you know about men?

ORIEL: Arnica will help the bruising, Mrs Pickles. And I'll give you a bit of liver for the eye.

DOLLY: No you won't.

ORIEL: You need looking after. Come and I'll clean you up.

DOLLY: Don't you reckon you've done enough good for one day?

She pushes ORIEL *away and goes.* ORIEL *runs to the Clay shop, finds* MRS CLAY *packing up.*

MRS CLAY: What do you want?

ORIEL: I came to talk to your husband.

MRS CLAY: Well, he's gone. That'll deprive youse all of a laugh.

ORIEL: Where's he gone to?

MRS CLAY: It's a big state. Anywhere he likes, I'd say.

ORIEL: I was here to offer him a settlement. What's he left you to live on?

MRS CLAY: Nothin'. Not a bent penny.

ORIEL: You need a job. Come and work with us. There's room in the house. You could bring the children.

MRS CLAY: Go away.

ORIEL: I'm offering you a job, a home.

MRS CLAY: And I'm tellin' you to go to Hell.
ORIEL: I'm sorry.
MRS CLAY: Go to Hell!

> MRS CLAY *goes.*

SCENE 40

Pelican Point. TED *is with a slightly older girl,* MARY.

TED: You look like someone off the pictures.
MARY: Pull the other one, Ted Pickles.
TED: Swear to God.

> *He tries to fondle her breasts.*

Specially right around here.
MARY: Get out of it.
TED: Come on, Mary. Take me while you got the chance.
MARY: Where are you off to?
TED: Dunno. But I'm gonna be a jockey.
MARY: Good in the saddle, are you?
TED: I can ride like blazes, yeah.
MARY: You're too young for me, Teddy.
TED: I'm sixteen.

> *She laughs with scorn.*

Fifteen.

> *She looks at him steadily.*

I'll be fifteen.
MARY: That's way too young.
TED: I'm old where it counts, Mary. Please.
MARY: Oh, Jesus... Go on.

> *She lets him touch her breasts.*

TED: Holy shit...

> *He goes to it.*

MARY: Now you tell me you love me.
TED: You got nice tits.
MARY: Is that all?
TED: This is going to change my life.
MARY: Likewise.

SCENE 41

QUICK *returns from school, ignoring* FISH.

QUICK: Quick's sixteen now, and bigger than his father. He tries to forget the pictures stuck on his wall. He thinks they're stupid now. At school he never speaks. He has to do an essay about the war. He writes about the atom bomb, says the Japs had it coming to them, it served them right. It was either us or them, writes Quick. Us or them. His teacher tells him Japanese people are more than just combustible material, and gives him a magazine with a long story about Hiroshima. Quick stares at photographs of what seem to be burnt logs, but when he looks close he sees the features of people. He takes the magazine home, but he's not going to read it...

FISH *plays the piano.* ROSE *watches him.*

ROSE: He's big now, Fish. Fourteen and growing like a man. Rose can't see the look on his face. She listens to him playing and wants only to touch him, to be friendly, and, yes, if she's honest, to get a kiss. It's ridiculous. She's too old for him, and he's a slowbo and a tenant, and a Lamb, for God's sake, but he's the grousest looking boy, and his hot, blue eyes make her go racy inside. She'd like to steal him and run away with him.

ROSE *leaves the room.*

Rose has her periods now, and hates her scrawny body. The minute she forces a bit of food into her, she runs outside and chucks it up. She watches those Lamb girls next door growing up. Hattie, the eldest, she starts going out to dances. Boys come to pick her up and off she goes. Elaine might like to be asked out too, but she gets a lot of headaches so she stays home. Red looks like she'd deck a boy if he came near her. Rose doesn't know any boys. Still, she's always got school.

DOLLY *finds her reading.*

DOLLY: Always got your head in a book, what's wrong with you?
ROSE: I got homework to do. Go away.
DOLLY: You shouldn't hate me. It doesn't help.
ROSE: Didn't you hate your mother?

DOLLY: Okay, you hate me, let's leave it at that.

ROSE: I've got an essay to write.

DOLLY: What for? We're not gonna keep you in school, anyway.

ROSE: What?

DOLLY: We're broke. We haven't got a brass razoo.

ROSE: I wonder why. What you don't drink the old man gives to the bookies.

DOLLY: Don't you backchat me, girl, or I'll give you one. You're old enough to be out working.

ROSE: But I want to stay at school.

DOLLY: People can't do everything they want to. Get yourself a job. It'll help us all out.

ROSE: Oh, anything to help out, Mum. Should I still do the cooking and the cleaning, or will you be getting someone else in?

DOLLY: You know, it's hate that keeps you so bloody skinny.

ROSE: No, hate keeps me going. Hating you is the best part of being alive.

DOLLY goes. ROSE packs up her schoolbooks.

SCENE 42

QUICK *is in his room. He picks up the magazine, puts it down, picks it up again.*

BLACK MAN: 'By nightfall thousands of victims of the explosion were moaning in the streets, surrounded by charred bodies...'

QUICK *puts it aside.*

QUICK: Bullshit. Stands to reason, it was us or them.

He opens it again.

BLACK MAN: 'A small child with the flesh seared off his face cried for his mother, who lay dead...'

QUICK *throws the magazine away. In the backyard* FISH *watches* LESTER *put up a guy.* LON, HAT, ELAINE *and* RED *bring kindling.*

FISH: What you doing, Lestah?

LESTER: We'll set this bloke on fire and have a real old party and a sing-song. It's Guy Fawkes Night!

FISH: Fire?

> ORIEL *sees* DOLLY, SAM, TED *and* CHUB *watching.*

ORIEL: Come on, Mrs Pickles. Lester's gone out and bought all the gear for the kids. They'd love it. Come on over. There's spuds to go in the fire and cakes and everywhatall.

DOLLY: We haven't got any crackers.

ORIEL: Plenty to go round. Bring the whole tribe. They'll love it!

LESTER: Come on, Sam. Time we all had a get-together.

DOLLY: No, thanks.

TED: I'm goin' out.

DOLLY: Teddy knows where to find his own crackers, don't you, love?

> TED *goes.*

CHUB: Look at all that tucker.

DOLLY: I'm not that hungry.

> *She goes.*

SAM: We're coming over, Lester. Rose!

CHUB: She won't come. She hates a good time.

> SAM *and* CHUB *join the* LAMBS. ROSE *is alone.* QUICK *has the magazine.* LESTER *calls from the yard.*

LESTER: Quick? Quick? Come on, we're going to light the guy.

ORIEL: Quick? We can't do it till everyone's here. Quick!

> QUICK *closes the magazine and goes into the yard.* LESTER *sets fire to the guy.*

LON: Whacko!

LESTER: Whacko! Strike up the band!

ORIEL: Whacko!

FISH: No! Burn the man. Don't burn him. He's the man.

> *He rages uncontrollably.*

RED: It's only grass, Fish. It's not a man.

FISH: You burn the man!

ORIEL: I'll give you a hiding if you don't slack off, son.

QUICK: The piano, Mum. Give him the piano.

> *He drags* FISH *to the piano then escapes to his own room.* ORIEL *finds him.*

43

ORIEL: Quick? You got to stay with Fish, son.

QUICK: Why me?

ORIEL: Because… because he sees you. He needs you. Now go and look after him!

She goes. QUICK *hears the piano.* ROSE *watches* FISH.

ROSE: Fish, are you all right? Fish?

FISH *plays on.* QUICK *packs gear in a duffle bag.*

QUICK: Mum, I'm goin'.

ORIEL: Going where?

QUICK: Goin'. I'm leavin' home. I'm old enough.

ORIEL: Go over to the sink and wash your mouth out with soap.

QUICK: I'm goin' bush, Mum. I didn't think you'd appreciate me doin' a bunk and not explainin'.

ORIEL: You're not going anywhere!

QUICK: You can't stop me, Mum.

LESTER *starts a song in the yard.*

LESTER: You put your left foot in… [etc.]

ORIEL: You've got no money, no trade.

QUICK: Mum, I'm going.

ORIEL: No! What about Fish? What'll happen to Fish?

QUICK: Let me go, Mum.

He runs out, knocking over ROSE *with his bag.*

[*To* ROSE] You're too bloody skinny!

He runs out of Cloudstreet. ORIEL *goes out to the party. She whispers something to* LESTER. *The party stops.*

SAM: What is it, Lest? The bum dropped out of the world?

LESTER: More or less, Sam. More or less.

END OF PART ONE

PART TWO

SCENE 43

ORIEL: On New Years' Day 1949, people gather to watch Oriel Lamb moving her things out of the house and pitching a white canvas tent under the mulberry tree in the backyard. She takes everything. Bed. Desk. Tilley lamp. Chamber-pot. Books. She's had enough kids, say the women in the street. She caught him out, say the blokes. But the real reason remains a mystery. Nobody knows why she's done it, not even Oriel.

She goes into the tent. Her shadow is visible.

SCENE 44

FISH *sits in a bath.* LESTER *brings towel and soap.*

FISH: No Quick. He's gone. He didn't say. You should say. Want to go in the boat with Quick.
LESTER: Quick isn't here, boy.
FISH: We seed the stars. Up in the water.
LESTER: Quick's gone away for a while, Fish.
FISH: I want the water, Lestah.
LESTER: I'll take you down to the river sometime, son.
FISH: Up in the boat. Up in the water.
LESTER: You can have a boat in the yard. Would you like that, mate? With oars and everything. What do you say?

Silence.

What's your name?
FISH: Fish.
LESTER: Fish who?
FISH: Fish Lamb.

LESTER: What's your proper name?

FISH: Samson.

LESTER: Who's your mum?

Silence.

Who's your mum? Who's the lady in the tent?

Silence.

Your dad?

FISH: You, Less.

LESTER: Sisters?

FISH: Red and Hattie and Lane.

LESTER: Brothers?

FISH: Quick Lamb.

LESTER: You forgot one.

FISH: Fish Lamb.

LESTER: One more. Small.

FISH: Lon. That Lon. The baby.

LESTER: He's a grown boy now, Fish. Where do you live?

FISH: Cloudstreet. The big house.

LESTER: That's right. You're clever enough, cobber. Want to sing a song?

FISH: The house sad, Lestah.

LESTER: How do you know that?

FISH: It talks. It hurts.

LESTER *kisses him.* FISH *stares at the bath.*

Lestah, more water, Lestah?

LESTER: Can only give you a little bit, Fish. 'Cause when it's deeper, you try and get under it.

FISH: No.

LESTER: Yes, you do.

Silence.

FISH: Do stories?

LESTER: No. I'm all out of stories, Fish. I can't even work up a decent joke.

FISH: The farm ones, Lestah. Stories!

LESTER: All right. Well...

He can't think of any.

FISH: Lest! Lestah!

LESTER: There was this boy. And he lived on a farm. Actually, this is me, it's the first thing I remember in my life. It was last century. It was night and my father was carrying me across a flooded creek. I was on his shoulders and could see the swirling darkness below. I was holding onto his ears and gripping his neck between my knees and—

FISH: Lestaah! Fish. Fish.

LESTER: All right, and there was this boy called Fish.

FISH: Hah!

LESTER: And he lived on a farm with only his brother.

FISH: Quick! Whacko, Lest!

LESTER: Yeah, with Quick. Everyone else was gone on holidays. One night it started to rain, see, and it came down like all of Heaven was tryin' to get in the roof. It rained and rained until the creek bust its banks. Pretty soon there was water in the lounge and water under the beds. So Quick wakes Fish up and tells him they got to go. They have to try and make it into town. Now Quick is bigger than Fish. He helps him into his clothes and holds his hand as they wade out into the water. There's rain peltin' down and it's dark. Quick puts Fish up on his shoulders and he strides into the water. It's a swirling torrent—

FISH: Yeah. And the water. Yes. They go inside the water. To the big country. Yeah.

LESTER: No, that's not what happens—

FISH: And people there for them. There's people there.

LESTER: Oh, God.

FISH: I miss Quick, Dad.

SCENE 45

Cloudstreet. Pickles side. Morning. ROSE, *dressed up as best she knows how, hurries off.*

SAM: Where you going, Rosie?

ROSE: None of your business.

SAM: You look grand. Like Ingrid Bergman.

ROSE: Shut up, Dad.

She goes. A big hairy MAN *in a blue singlet approaches.*

SAM: G'day. How can—?

The MAN *knocks him to the ground and pushes his face into the earth.*

MAN: My daughter's up the duff, Pickles, and your boy's gettin' married. All right?

SAM: Which one?

MAN: I've only got one.

SAM: Boy. Which boy are we talkin' about?

The MAN *lifts* SAM *off the ground.*

MAN: Don't play funny buggers with me, mate. Ted or Todd or whatever his bloody name is, he's going to do the right thing. I'm not askin' and I'm not makin' requests, you get my drift?

LESTER *appears with a bloody meat cleaver in his hand. The* MAN *backs away from* SAM.

LESTER: What's going on here?

MAN: Shit! Let's go easy in this particular vicinity.

SAM: He's a mad bastard. Be careful!

He holds up his stump. The MAN's *eyes widen.*

Look what he did to me, for Chrissake! You tell me where you live and I'll be round with my boy. We'll sort it out.

MAN: Whatever you say, mate...

He slides away.

LESTER: He a friend of yours, Sam?

SAM: No, but you are, sport. Take a week's free rent from me. [*Calling*] Ted! [*To* LESTER] What would you've done with that cleaver there?

LESTER: I'm choppin' bones for soup. It's cheaper than a bone saw.

SAM: Must be me with the brain damage. [*Calling*] Ted! [*To* LESTER] Can I borrow that sometime?

LESTER: Course. What you cutting?

SAM: Thinkin' about what them Jews do. Bit of circum-whatsit.

LESTER: You? You going to…?

SAM: Not me, cobber. My eldest. And I tell you, my hand'll be none too steady. He'll be sittin' down to piss. Ted! I tell you, Lester, never have kids.

LESTER: Yeah… what?

DOLLY *appears, hung over, as* LESTER *goes back inside.*

DOLLY: What's up with you?

SAM: It's your Ted. We're going to have to sort him out.

DOLLY: That'll be the day. Ted's the only one round here with anything goin' for him.

CHUB *comes out, eating.*

CHUB: You're wastin' your breath, Dad, he's shot through.

SAM: What are you talking about?

CHUB: He's upped and gone. Taken all his gear.

DOLLY: What?

CHUB: Look in the bedroom! He's pissed off. Gunna be a jockey.

SAM: Ted got some piece up the duff, Doll. That's why he's gone, the chicken-livered little rooster.

DOLLY: Gone?

SAM: I reckon.

SAM *goes inside.* CHUB *goes off.*

DOLLY: Teddy?

SCENE 46

Baird's store, Perth. MRS TISBORNE*'s office.*

MRS TISBORNE: No previous employment?

ROSE: None that paid, Mrs Tisborne.

MRS TISBORNE: What makes you want to work for us?

ROSE: You want a straight answer, or one that might get me the job?

MRS TISBORNE: The latter.

ROSE: Baird's is a great Perth institution and it would be a real honour for a girl to work in such gracious surroundings.

MRS TISBORNE: Charming. Now the straight answer.

ROSE: I hate being stuck at home. I want to meet some people, I mean people I'm not related to. I want to live a bit and—

49

MRS TISBORNE: That's enough.

ROSE *starts to leave.*

You should start as an office girl, and work your way up. But you can talk and you can think, and I'm prepared to try you out on the switchboard.

ROSE: Thank you very much, Mrs Tisborne.

MRS TISBORNE: Don't be grateful and don't be late. You can start tomorrow morning. You're dreadfully thin. Don't they feed you at home?

ROSE: I feed myself.

MRS TISBORNE: Then do it more regularly.

MRS TISBORNE *goes. A switchboard appears.* ROSE *joins* DARLEEN, MERLE *and* ALMA, *all with headsets.*

ALMA: Good morning, Baird's.

DARLEEN: Did old Teasebone give you the runaround, love? You'll be right. You'll put a hurdle in her girdle, won't she, girls? What was your name again? Good morning, Baird's.

ROSE: Rose.

DARLEEN: Connecting you now. I'm Darleen.

MERLE: Merle.

ALMA: Alma.

ROSE: Darleen, Merle, Alma. What do I do?

The GIRLS *demonstrate at speed.*

DARLEEN: 'Good morning, Baird's, can I help you?'

MERLE: The caller asks for a department. 'Connecting you now.' Make the connection, like so...

ALMA: If this light shows the line is busy, ask 'Will you hold?'

DARLEEN: 'Thank you, sir or madam.'

MERLE: 'Up your bum, sir or madam.'

ALMA: It's dead simple, Rose. Follow us. You shove the Jacks into the Jills. Like so. Remind you of anything? Eh?

DARLEEN: Good morning, Baird's. One moment, sir. Jack into Jill...

MERLE: Good morning, Baird's. Jack into Jill...

ROSE: Good morning, Baird's. Jack into Jill...

SCENE 47

Dusk. A truck spotlight scans wheat fields.

BLACK MAN: Quick lets the roos come into the clearing before he turns the spot on them. They go rigid and open their eyes to him. Quick works them left to right without haste. Shoot, load, aim, shoot. The roos stand there, unable to tear themselves away. Shoot, load, aim, shoot... Shoot, load, aim, shoot... Then Quick hears a noise, a gasping noise from the wheat. 'I missed one', he thinks. 'Poor bugger's out there chokin'.'

> QUICK *is knocked over by a wounded roo.*

Quick hears the sound of blood marching across him, establishing a beachhead on his chest. He watches the spotlight on the ute fade as the battery juices out. He sees the Southern Cross melt into the darkness. If he can't walk, he'll die out here. In a moment he'll have to try. No use putting it off. Bound to be able to walk. Light comes across the sky, a great Saint Elmo's fire of a thing, turning and twisting, till it fishtails towards the earth and is gone.

> FISH *rows over the wheat, hovering over* QUICK.

QUICK: Fish?... Fish?... I'm under it, mate. I'm under water, under something. God Almighty, I'm gonna drown.

FISH: Come on, Quick, let's go fishin'.

QUICK: Fish? Am I all right?

FISH: Come on, Quick.

QUICK: I can't.

FISH: Quick?

QUICK: I can't. I can't!

FISH: You love me?

QUICK: Yes! Yeah, Fish. But I just can't move. Where you goin', Fish? You goin' home?

FISH: The Big Country.

> *He rows away.*

QUICK: Fish!

SCENE 48

QUICK *wakes in a bed at a homestead.* MR WENTWORTH *is beside him, with* LUCY.

WENTWORTH: You're bloody lucky a man was goin' by on the off-chance. You would have died sure as shit, I reckon. You'll have to stay here till you're back on your feet.

QUICK: Very kind of you.

WENTWORTH: I don't give anything away, son. Not even kindness. I'll charge you a week's cull for room and board. This is my daughter Lucy. She'll look after you.

He leaves LUCY *with* QUICK.

LUCY: You had us worried, Quick Lamb. Must have lost a bucket of blood out there. Still, the doctor reckons you'll pull through. God, you got yourself burnt, but. I can feel the heat comin' off you in waves. Never mind, I'll fix you up.

QUICK: What's that?

LUCY: Goanna oil. Takes the sting out.

QUICK: Thanks.

LUCY: How come you never been round to see me?

QUICK: 'Scuse me?

LUCY: All the other fellas come sniffing around, giving it a try, not that I'd look twice at any of 'em, pack of no-hopers. You, you've been in the district three years and never come near me.

QUICK: I like living bush by myself.

LUCY: Why's that?

QUICK: I come from a big family, that's why.

They both smile.

LUCY: Is that really your name? Quick Lamb?

QUICK: Yeah.

LUCY: Because you're fast?

Her hand goes under the sheet.

QUICK: No.

She grabs his dick.

I didn't get burnt down there.

LUCY: It's all right, Quick.

She starts to jerk him off.

Heard a lot about you.

QUICK: Yeah?

LUCY: Cockies reckon you're the best shot the district's ever seen.

QUICK: I... I've got my mum's eyes. Long-distance eyes...

LUCY: Is this your first time? It is, isn't it? You're blushin'.

QUICK: It's sunburn.

LUCY: Yeah, but you just went red in the white bits. You've got a huge whanger, Quick. I like that on a man. [*She looks under the covers.*] A head like that, it ought to be eligible to vote.

He gives in to the experience.

I'm going to live in Perth. I'm gonna have a flower shop. A floristry.

QUICK: Mmngh?

LUCY: My dad's gonna set me up...

QUICK: Hhhyeah?

LUCY: Though he doesn't exactly know it yet.

QUICK: Hhhhow long have you planned to do that?

LUCY: I just thought of it. Three minutes ago. I got it all figured out. I like the smell of flowers.

QUICK *comes.*

SCENE 49

Morning. ROSE *is by herself on the switch.*

ROSE: Baird's, good morning.

TOBY'S VOICE: Hmm. Baird's.

ROSE: Can I help you, sir?

TOBY'S VOICE: It's about Earl Grey.

ROSE: Does he work here, sir? The name's not familiar.

TOBY'S VOICE: It's tea, love.

ROSE: Mr T. Earl Gray, is it?

TOBY'S VOICE: Oh, a card, are you?

ROSE: Sir?

TOBY'S VOICE: I'm expecting some tea from you people and it's weeks overdue.

ROSE: I'll give you to Mail Order, then, sir. Gladly.

53

She unplugs TOBY.

Good morning, Baird's. Connecting you now, ma'am. Earl flamin' Grey, my bum! Good morning—

TOBY'S VOICE: I heard that. I should report you, girlie.

ROSE: The firing squad in haberdashery or death by moron on the switch, it's all the same to me, mate.

TOBY'S VOICE: Now, listen here!

ROSE: There's a ladder in your stockings, sir. I'll give you Haberdashery and Hosiery.

TOBY'S VOICE: No, no—

She unplugs him.

ROSE: Good morning, Baird's. Manchester? One moment. [*She answers another call.*] Good morning, Baird's.

TOBY'S VOICE: It's me again.

ROSE: You don't say. Any luck with Earl?

TOBY'S VOICE: They haven't found him yet.

ROSE: Dear, dear. Want me to put you through to the Governor-General?

TOBY'S VOICE: You're a cheeky bugger.

ROSE: Thanks a dozen, but I've got to get back to work. There's a lot of buggerizing to be done.

TOBY'S VOICE: Well, I'm going to keep after this tea.

ROSE: Good luck, Earl.

DARLEEN, MERLE *and* ALMA *arrive late.* ROSE *unplugs* TOBY. *They go to work.*

Baird's, good morning... Putting you through... I had the Charge of the Light Brigade on my hands here. Where the hell have youse been?

DARLEEN: Oh, a meetin' of minds in William Street.

ROSE: Sailors, I suppose.

DARLEEN: How'd you guess?

ROSE: Who else is gonna go you three in a group at nine o'clock in the morning? They must've been at sea a good while to pick a pack of rough sheilas like you. Baird's, good morning.

ALMA: Merle's sailor's a dwarf. Baird's, good morning.

MERLE: Good morning, Baird's... You're a liar, she's lyin'.

ALMA: Putting you through. He's shorter than Mum's pastry!

DARLEEN: Short ones have got fat thingies. Good morning, Baird's.

ALMA: Well, she's hardly the eye of the needle. One moment, Madam.

ROSE: Youse sheilas are gettin' fouler every day. Baird's, good morning.

TOBY'S VOICE: Hello. Listen, why don't we meet somewhere? You sound like a smart girl.

ROSE: Only meet smart ones, do you?

TOBY'S VOICE: What about lunch?

ROSE: Let's meet at the GPO. First column on the left as you go up the stairs. Twelve o'clock. Bring your teapot.

> ROSE *hangs up.*

SCENE 50

TOBY *waits at the GPO.* ROSE *approaches.*

ROSE: Mr T. Earl Grey. Hope you haven't strained yourself.

TOBY: Hello. I thought you'd be a looker.

ROSE: You hungry? I am.

TOBY: Yes, yes, let's get a bite.

> *They walk together.*

I'll guess, and you tell me how close I am. You left school at fifteen. Your dad votes Labor, you play netball, you'd like to be a lawyer's secretary and you sleep with your socks on.

ROSE: Patchy, but boring enough to get me right.

TOBY: What's your name?

ROSE: Rosemary.

TOBY: Do you like Rose?

ROSE: Yes.

TOBY: My name's Toby Raven, by the way.

> *Silence.*

What a talker. Do you need the switchboard between us before you really fire?

ROSE: I suppose so. Suddenly I don't know what to talk about.

TOBY: Football? The common cold?

ROSE: Just ask me out.

TOBY: Let's go out Friday.

ROSE: Now I'll guess. You went to uni, your parents live in Nedlands but you've tried to teach yourself to talk like one of us.

She starts walking away.

TOBY: Us? Where you going?

ROSE: I'll see you Friday.

TOBY: Give me your address. I'll pick you up.

ROSE: No! I'll meet you somewhere.

TOBY: It's no trouble. Where do you live?

ROSE: Meet me at Shenton Park Station. Seven o'clock. 'Bye.

SCENE 51

BLACK MAN: One night as Quick waits for the roos, he hears the familiar bashing in the wheat and raises the rifle and hits the spotlight to get a look at the bugger. But it's a man; he sees a man running raw and shirtless in the light. And it's him, right there in the cross-hairs of his Lee-Enfield.

QUICK *shines the roo light across the wheat. A figure freezes in the spotlight, then runs away.*

His finger itches for first pressure on the trigger. He sees himself running. He sits back, rolls a smoke and thinks: thank God I didn't shoot.

FISH: Who's the man, Quick?

QUICK: Every few nights, it happens again. He'll hit the light and sees himself tearing out into the open, right in the sights. It scares the skin off him.

QUICK *and* LUCY *drive in* QUICK's *ute.*

LUCY: What's up with you tonight?

QUICK: Nothin'.

LUCY: Make a killin' this week, did you?

QUICK: No I didn't.

LUCY: Must be losin' your eye. Quick Lamb. Crack shot.

QUICK: I haven't shot a week's worth this whole month.

LUCY: Crack shot. Make you think of anything?

QUICK: You don't have to talk like that.

LUCY: Oh. I forgot you went to church.

QUICK: You shouldn't push me, Luce. I take a lot of crap from you.

LUCY: You get a lot of other things, too. What other girls you got in town like me?

QUICK: What others are there, full stop? Geez, you haven't got much competition.

LUCY: Suppose you feel sorry for me.

QUICK: Suppose I do. A bit.

LUCY: Well, you shouldn't. You think I'm a... a conquest?

QUICK: No. I never went after you.

LUCY: You come by every Saturday night, mate. Isn't that comin' after me?

QUICK: You asked me to, once.

LUCY: Oh, you've just been obedient these last six months?

QUICK: Reckon I have been.

LUCY: You bloody bastard! You thought your dick was for cleanin' your rifle before I took you in.

QUICK: Did you take me in?

LUCY: What do you reckon? I reckon we could make a go of it, you and me. Don't you reckon?

QUICK: I don't see myself stayin' out here, Lucy.

LUCY: Me neither. I see myself in the city. In my flower shop.

QUICK *stops the ute and gets out.*

Hey, Quick, you're not... are you?

QUICK: What?

LUCY: Leavin' me here? I thought you were gonna leave me out here.

She climbs out.

QUICK: I want some air, and while I'm out here I reckon I'll take a piss, all right?

He starts trying to pee.

LUCY: Quick, we shouldn't fight. I'm good for you, mate. I got big plans.

QUICK: For your flower shop?

LUCY: That's right. And more. Without me you're a duck, Quick. Just a sittin' duck. You're dumber than a post.

QUICK: Reckon I am.

LUCY: Can't you go?

QUICK: Leave off, will you? Lucy, I just don't see the two of us...
You know what I'm sayin'?

LUCY: I reckon...

They hear the sound of a distant car. LUCY *strips off her skirt.*
She's naked except for her bobby socks.

QUICK: Lucy?! What are you doing?! Get your gear back on!

The headlights find them.

LUCY: Now you may kiss the bride.

SCENE 52

Perth. TOBY*'s flat.*

ROSE: You've got a view.

TOBY: Not what I'd call a real view. Did you enjoy yourself?

ROSE: I've never met someone with so many friends.

TOBY: They're not exactly friends.

ROSE: Well... all those people in the restaurant.

TOBY: I know who they are and they know who I am. I suppose I'm
clubbish. It's my last concession to a bourgeois past. Would you
like a drink? I've got some brandy.

ROSE: The wine was enough. I've never had wine before. Or spaghetti.

TOBY: Bit of a change from mutton and boiled veg, eh?

ROSE: It was nice.

TOBY: Are you okay? Don't be nervous. I'm quite safe, you know.
Not respectable but I am able to restrain myself with a lady.

ROSE: Look at the lights on the river. They're nice.

TOBY: Nice? This is one of the world's strangest towns.

ROSE: I wouldn't know.

TOBY: Perth is the most isolated country town in the world trying to
be a city. Desert on one side, sea on the other. There's something
nesting here, something horrible waiting. Ambition, Rose. It
squeezes us into corners and turns out ugly shapes. What are you
thinking now?

ROSE: We're different.

TOBY: How?

ROSE: I'm a switchgirl and you're a writer. And you've been to uni.
That makes us different.

TOBY: And…

> *He moves closer.*

ROSE: What do you write?

TOBY: If you could call it writing. I'm a journalist on the *Daily*. A hack. I scribble a bit of poetry in my own time. Do you read?

ROSE: Yes, I read.

TOBY: Thank God, she reads. See, we're not so different. Tell me who you read.

ROSE: Oh, God.

TOBY: Don't be shy.

ROSE: I read the whole Geraldton library end-to-end when I was a kid.

TOBY: Name some names.

ROSE: You name some.

TOBY: Hammett, Steinbeck, Hemingway, James Jones, Mailer, D. H. Lawrence, Xavier Herbert, Sillitoe, Camus…

> *He gets closer. They kiss.*

ROSE: I like talking about books. It's nice.

TOBY: Nice is a terrible, bourgeois word.

ROSE: Oh. Sorry.

TOBY: Don't be sorry for anything.

> *He kisses her again.*

ROSE: Well… Just switching you through.

> TOBY *starts to make love to her.*

SCENE 53

QUICK: Lucy is beside herself with happiness. She's got her ticket out of town. She begins negotiations with her father for a flower shop. But Quick can't hang around. It's not that he doesn't like her. He never minded wrestling around with her, and having her grabbers in his shorts. But he's never thought about her much. So he packs up the Dodge and heads off.

> QUICK *drives the truck alone. A* BLACK MAN *in a pinstriped suit with a Gladstone bag, holds his thumb out.* QUICK *doesn't stop. Magically, the* BLACK MAN *reappears.* QUICK *pulls over and opens the door.*

BLACK MAN: Ta.

He climbs into the ute.

QUICK: Weren't you just... back there?

BLACK MAN: No.

QUICK *looks at him for a moment and drives on.*

QUICK: Wanna smoke?

BLACK MAN: Yeah. Ta. Hungry?

QUICK: Yeah, I could do with a bite.

From his bag, the BLACK MAN *pulls out bread and a bottle.*

Whacko. [QUICK *speaks to the audience.*] They drive all night.
And the fuel gauge never goes down. Something drags Quick on,
drags him forward, but he doesn't know what. He's been going
along without any feeling for so long, without caring either way,
he doesn't know what to feel now. So Quick keeps driving. [*To
the* BLACK MAN] How we doing for time?

BLACK MAN: Well as can be expected.

QUICK: Where you from, mate?

BLACK MAN: All over.

QUICK: I mean, where's your family?

BLACK MAN: All over.

QUICK: That's a nice suit. Never seen an Aborigine in a pinstripe
before. You must have a bit of a job.

BLACK MAN: Bit of a job.

QUICK: Family business?

BLACK MAN: Always family business.

QUICK: Headin' for the city?

The BLACK MAN *nods. And* QUICK *smiles to himself.*

Family business...

FISH *appears above them again.*

FISH: Who's the man, Quick? Who's the man?

QUICK *slows the truck and looks at the* BLACK MAN.

QUICK: Where can I drop you?

BLACK MAN: Just follow the railway line a bit further.

QUICK: Any place in particular?

As he slows the ute, the BLACK MAN *points.*

BLACK MAN: Just up there a bit. Corner of Cloud Street, mate.

QUICK: No... I... I'll drop you here.

The BLACK MAN *gets out, looks back at* QUICK.

BLACK MAN: Comin'?

QUICK: No.

QUICK *throws the truck into gear, leaving the* BLACK MAN *behind.*

FISH: Come home, brother boy. Come home.

SCENE 54

Margaret River. COUSIN FRED *at work sees* QUICK *approaching.*

QUICK: Fred Blunt. I'm your cousin.

COUSIN FRED: One of Lester's boys. Mason.

QUICK: They call me Quick. You still doin' haulage?

COUSIN FRED *nods.*

I need a bed and a job.

COUSIN FRED: You're in luck. I need another driver.

QUICK: I'm on.

COUSIN FRED: How's the family?

QUICK: I wouldn't know. When do I start?

COUSIN FRED: Now. Come on.

SCENE 55

Lamb side. Night. LESTER *finds* ORIEL *in her tent.*

LESTER: Orry? Will you come out of that tent?

ORIEL: What is it, Lester?

LESTER: Nothing. Just felt like a bit of a talk.

ORIEL: What about?

LESTER: Does it have to be about something?

ORIEL: It'd help.

LESTER: Well... Quick. Do you think we'll ever hear from Quick?

ORIEL: I wouldn't hold your breath. For goodness sake, what's up?

LESTER: I don't know. Life throws a million things, good and bad, at me. I just wish I knew what to believe in.

ORIEL: You believe in what you like, Lester Lamb. That's one thing I can't show you.

LESTER: You've got hard, Oriel.

ORIEL: It's the war that's done it to me.

LESTER: The war's been over for years.

ORIEL: Not that war. The big one. Raising a family. Keeping your head above water. Life. It's all war.

LESTER: Well, struggle, maybe.

ORIEL: No, no, it's war.

LESTER: Ah, things come along. You take the good with the bad.

ORIEL: I won't stand for the bad. Bad people, bad luck, bad ways, not even bad breath. We make good, Lester. We make war on the bad and don't surrender.

LESTER: Some things can't be helped.

ORIEL: Everything can be helped.

LESTER: You're a hard woman to please, Oriel.

ORIEL: That's what I tell myself.

LESTER: Aren't you happy?

ORIEL: Do I look like a winner?

LESTER: We have a place to live in. We're three years ahead with the rent, the kids have food and clothes, they go to school and have jobs. And there's the shop. People say: There goes Mrs Lamb, who lives in a tent. She runs the best shop this side of the river. You're famous! Course you're a winner.

ORIEL: A winner wins them all, Lester, not just the worldly things.

LESTER: You've won me, love.

ORIEL: You're a fool, Lester Lamb.

LESTER: That's what I tell myself.

He puts a hand on her leg.

Do you still love me?

ORIEL: I married you before God.

She goes back towards the tent.

LESTER: Oriel? Why do you live in that tent?

ORIEL: Why did Quick run away? Why is Fish the way he is? Why does this house... behave?

LESTER: I used to ride farm to farm down there at Margaret, and I'd look out across the hills. The whole flamin' country looked sad. And you know, I used to hear it moan. Not the wind. The ground, the land. I told myself it was the horse, but inside I knew it was the country. Moanin'.

ORIEL: Like this house.

LESTER: I thought it was just me hearin' it. You think maybe we don't belong here, like we're out of our depth, out of our country?

ORIEL: We don't belong anywhere. When I was a girl I had this strong feeling I didn't belong, not in my body, not on the land. It was in my head, what I thought and dreamt, what I believed, Lester, that's where I belonged, that was my country. That was the final line of defence in the war.

LESTER: What you sayin', love?

ORIEL: Since Fish... I've been losing the war. I've lost my bearings. All I can do is work.

LESTER: You believe in work, love.

ORIEL: Not for its own sake, I don't. We weren't born to work. Look at them next door.

LESTER: Well, you believe in the family.

ORIEL: Families aren't things you believe in, they're things you work with.

LESTER: Don't you believe in love?

ORIEL: No. I feel love. I'm stuck with the love I've got, and I'm trying to work with the love I haven't got. 'Do you believe in love?' he says. That's like saying 'do you believe in babies?' They happen.

LESTER: What about goodness, loving kindness, charity?

ORIEL: They're just things you do, you try to do. There's no point believin' in them.

LESTER: So what do you want?

ORIEL: I want to go inside that tent, lace it up and never come out. You could slip food under the flap and I'd never see a soul, never say a living word.

LESTER: Why?

ORIEL: Then I could get on with the real war.

LESTER: You want a miracle, don't you?

63

ORIEL: I want the miracle finished off. I demand it, and I'm gonna fight to get it.

LESTER: So you do believe.

ORIEL: Lester, I believe in eight hours' sleep and a big breakfast.

She goes into the tent.

SCENE 56

Cloudstreet. SAM *arrives home, bloodied and dishevelled.*

DOLLY: My God. That's what I call a day's work. What the Christ have you been into?

SAM: My luck's runnin' uphill.

DOLLY: Runnin' out your arse, by the look of you. You've lost a tooth.

SAM: Pack me a bag, love. I better disappear for a bit.

DOLLY: How much do you owe?

SAM: It's who I owe, Doll...

DOLLY: How many of them?

SAM: Just the one. One fella. Who owns all the fellas.

DOLLY: Oh, Gawd. Haven't you got some union mates to back you up?

SAM: They are the union.

DOLLY: Jesus.

She goes. LESTER *appears with cauliflowers.*

LESTER: G'day. I've got some old caulies. They'd be good for a soup.

He sees SAM'*s state.*

You all right?

SAM: Yeah, yeah, come in, Lester.

DOLLY *brings the bag.*

LESTER: Evening, Mrs Pickles. You off, then, Sam?

SAM: Yeah. I've got some business to do.

LESTER: You're in trouble. The bookies?

DOLLY: The union.

LESTER: Ah, the flamin' unions, is it? Need to find a bit of tin to crawl under, eh? I'll get the truck.

SCENE 57

ROSE *comes home as* LESTER *and* SAM *go.*

ROSE: He's in the poo, isn't he? I can always tell.
DOLLY: You look all right. You're filling out.
ROSE: Thanks. Listen, Mum—
DOLLY: Why are you home, anyway? Why aren't you out with that bloke, the smart-bum?
ROSE: How'd you know about him?
DOLLY: I know a lot more than you reckon. You haven't scared him off, have you?
ROSE: No, I've got the painters in, that's all. Mum—
DOLLY: God was laughing when he made women, eh?
ROSE: Mum, will you listen?
DOLLY: Don't go crook on me, I'm trying to be nice.
ROSE: Sorry. It's just... Ted rang me up at work today.
DOLLY: Ted? He rang you? Teddy never even liked you.
ROSE: He married a girl in Adelaide, and—
DOLLY: Married? When?
ROSE: A while ago, at least I hope so. They've just had a little boy.
DOLLY: I'm a grandmother. I'm old. I'm old.
ROSE: You're doing all right.
DOLLY: And he never even told his old mum about the wedding. I love a wedding. I'm a bloody grandmother.

She slides off on her own.

SCENE 58

LESTER *brings* SAM *to the beach shack. Each carries a crate.*

SAM: This is it? I didn't know you had a beach shack.
LESTER: One of the customers gives us the use of it, but somehow we never have the time. How long will you need?
SAM: A week maybe.
LESTER: Will it blow over or do you have to blow it over?
SAM: I reckon I have to do it myself. Trouble is, it'll cost money to blow it over.
LESTER: I can't lend you any, the wife wouldn't have it.

SAM: Wouldn't necessarily be a loan. Rent in advance, maybe.

LESTER: We're paid up for years already. How much do you owe?

SAM: Two hundred quid.

LESTER: Two hundred quid! Half a year's wages! Two hundred quid! You could buy—

SAM: Yeah, all right!

LESTER: No wonder they're punchy. Do those blokes know where you live?

SAM *nods.*

They'll come looking for you, won't they?

SAM *nods.*

No one'll find you out here. You stay put till I can bring you the money to pay them off. All right?

SAM: What's in it for you?

LESTER: It'll buy me some peace of mind. I won't have to worry about bruisers hangin' round my kids or my house.

He goes.

SCENE 59

Night. LESTER *finds* DOLLY *at Cloudstreet.*

DOLLY: Where is he?

LESTER: Up the coast a bit.

DOLLY: What am I supposed to do?

LESTER: Sit tight, I reckon. You've got some way of raisin' the money?

DOLLY: I could stand on the corner. That'd bring in enough for a packet of smokes... Sorry if I'm a bit rough for you.

She stares at LESTER. *He fidgets.*

What if they come after him?

LESTER: If they do, tell them to see me.

DOLLY: You don't seem the fightin' type, Lester.

LESTER: There won't be any fight.

DOLLY: How much is it, anyway?

LESTER: Two hundred pounds.

DOLLY: You can't have that kind of dough.

LESTER: There's savings we got. We live poor. We never buy anything, except for the shop.

DOLLY: You know it'll be money down the dunny.

He shrugs, mesmerised as she crosses her legs.

LESTER: What else am I supposed to do?

DOLLY: What do you mean?

LESTER: If this thing turned into a proper blue we might find ourselves on the street. What if you had to sell to clear your debts?

DOLLY: We can't. Not for years. It's in the deed.

LESTER: Then these blokes'd come around and take goods to the value of. Guess which end they'll pillage. I reckon it's worth me insurin' against that.

DOLLY: And that's all?

She kisses LESTER *full on the mouth.*

You sure that's all you're buyin'? A bit of safety?

They kiss again, deeply.

LESTER: It's like the Saturday Matinee.

DOLLY: What?

LESTER: The Saturday Matinee.

DOLLY: Well, listen to the popcorn goin' off between your ears.

LESTER *rears out of the chair. He fucks* DOLLY *on the table. In the shack* SAM *tosses a coin.*

SAM: Thirty. [*He flips again, checks.*] Thirty-one. [*He flips again, checks.*] Thirty-two. Thirty-two heads in a row. And Pickles, you prize dill, you didn't even call! I dunno if I'm winnin' or bloody losin'!

He tosses the coin again. LESTER *and* DOLLY *have just finished fucking.*

LESTER: Was that rape, do you think?

DOLLY: I suppose not. More like a deposit on two hundred quid.

LESTER *covers his face.*

You been waitin' years for that.

LESTER: And you?

DOLLY: I been waitin' all my life for everything.

LESTER: We're different.

DOLLY: Yeah. You're no oil painting, Lester, but you're a nice bloke. You've got a hundred and ninety quid's worth left.

LESTER: No.

DOLLY: Very flatterin', Lester.

LESTER: No, not to either of us.

DOLLY: You're a churchy bugger, mate. When you get what you're after you go off feelin' awful.

LESTER: And you just go off soundin' awful.

DOLLY: What d'you want, cobber?

LESTER: I want you not to use this against me.

DOLLY: I told you you weren't buyin' safety.

LESTER: Lester tries to get organised. But it's beyond him. It isn't the Saturday Matinee anymore. He goes to bed with the curtains drawn and sleeps till noon, paralysed with wondering how he could have got himself into such a spot. What has he done? What should he do now? Tell Oriel [about Sam's debt]? Or go behind her back, hand over their savings to keep his family safe at Cloudstreet? He notices how patched together everything is, everything in the house. What have they been saving for, anyway?

SCENE 60

LESTER *finds* SAM *still tossing a coin in the shack.*

SAM: About bloody time. Few more days and they'll be chookrafflin' me to the nuthouse. You got the money, then?

LESTER: Said I would.

SAM: Good on you. I'm feelin' lucky.

He scratches his back.

LESTER: What's wrong with your back?

SAM: Friggin' boils.

LESTER: When did they come up?

SAM: Today.

LESTER: Don't scratch 'em.

SAM: They're itchy.

LESTER: They're not boils you got there. It's tics. Roo tics.

SAM: Bugger me!

LESTER: Give me your smoke and pull up your singlet.

SAM: What are you gunna do, for Chrissake?

LESTER: Burn 'em out.

SAM: Wonderful. Bloody marvellous.

He hands his a cigarette to LESTER.

LESTER: You won't feel a thing except those little fellers reversin' out in a hurry.

SAM: My dad once de-carbuncled me. Laughin'. 'Ohh, I'll bung these on my toast tonight, son!' I tell you, Lester. I feel lucky.

LESTER: Oh, you look lucky.

SAM: There's a big two-up game tomorrow.

LESTER: Two-up? Don't be stupid!

SAM: You said you'd got the money.

LESTER: To pay off your debts and keep trouble away from Cloudstreet.

SAM: Well, I'm gunna do that and make us some money.

LESTER: Us?

SAM: Well, you're stakin' me. I reckon you're entitled to a dividend.

LESTER: You'll lose it, Sam.

SAM: Don't bloody talk like that. The Shadow's about. I know when I'm gunna win.

LESTER: I can't do it.

SAM: I'll toss you for it.

LESTER: This is no joke, Sam. Tell me who's after you, I'll go and pay them off right now.

SAM: You're gutless, Lamb. You got Sunday School written all over you. Carn, Lester. I'm gunna win. Me stump's bloody near glowin'. I know it.

LESTER: I deserve a horsewhippin'.

SAM: For what?

LESTER: For this... and a lot of other things. Here it is. Two hundred quid.

SAM: You're in?

LESTER: No, you're in.

They go.

SCENE 61

LESTER *comes home.* DOLLY *intercepts him.*

DOLLY: Well, where is he?
LESTER: Don't ask me.
DOLLY: What's up? You look like you just lost a quid and found a shillin'.
LESTER: I'll let you know when I find the shillin'.
DOLLY: Are you in the poo too?
LESTER: Let me put it this way, Mrs Pickles. By midnight we're probably all gunna be in the poo.
DOLLY: People like you aren't used to it.
LESTER: Being in trouble, you mean?
DOLLY: Yeah. What have you done?
LESTER: Oh, just put all our savings in a two-up game.
DOLLY: Why would you do that?
LESTER: Well, it's hard to deny a man a chance when you've...
DOLLY: When you've what?

>*He looks away.*

I suppose this means you won't be visiting again?

>*He goes. In a back alley* SAM *plays two-up. A cluster of* BLOKES *surround him as he tosses.*

SCENE 62

Cloudstreet. Night. ORIEL's *shadow can be seen as she reads her Bible alone in her tent.* HAT *returns from a dance.* RED *and* ELAINE *see her.*

ELAINE: How was Geoff?
HAT: Geoff's a dreamboat.
RED: Geoff's a mug, Hat. Face the fact.
HAT: He's asked me to marry him, that's how much of a mug he is.
RED: And you'll be a mug if you say yes.
ELAINE: You're getting married? Oh, my God...
HAT: Look, you just have to get out and meet some blokes, Ee. Then it'll happen for you. For the both of you.
RED: It won't happen for me, no fear.

ROSE *comes home from an evening out.*

ELAINE: There's Rose Pickles. She's seeing a bloke.

HAT: How do you know?

ELAINE: I can always tell. Someone posh, I reckon.

RED: How would you know!

ELAINE: 'Cause she never lets him come round here.

HAT: Geoff's coming round to see Dad tomorrow. He wants a quiet wedding. I know exactly what I'm going to wear.

ELAINE: God, my head. I need a Vincent's.

She goes with HAT. RED *lingers.*

RED: Had a nice night?

ROSE: Oh. Yes, thanks, Red.

RED: Your hair looks pretty. That dress is a good colour for you.

ROSE *sees the light in the tent.*

ROSE: Your mum's still up and about.

RED: She's a saint, you know. There's no one else like her alive. Rose... I'm going nursing next year.

ROSE: Oh, good.

RED: Well, goodnight.

They go their separate ways.

SCENE 63

Dawn. ORIEL *comes out of the tent.*

ORIEL: Oriel wakes, remembering her own bare running feet on the dirt of the home paddock when the world was a place given by God for the pleasures of children, when all that was good was unbroken. Then she remembers how all that was broken. She knows that one day soon Hat will be getting married, leaving another hole in the company. Another loss. If Oriel thinks about everything that's been taken from her over the years... The mother who died and left her to bring up a family, the brother shot by a Turkish bullet, and now her own sons... Lord, it's like the longest subtraction sum invented.

She can't help it, the feeling is on her and she's furious. It's a sickness, self-pity, it'll eat the day and worm into your labour and weaken you.

71

Sometimes she wakes dreaming of hell. She's six years old, and alone in the dark, the only one left. She comes out of the tent and runs to the house and goes from room to room checking that all of them are still there, that it's not only her left again. All of them breathing in their beds, helpless and sweet in sleep. She sits on Quick's empty bed while Fish snores. She looks in on Lester. There's no malice in the man, you have to give him that, and she still loves him. Yes, there's a hell, there are hells abounding, and if there's not a heaven, there's this, the sleeping, the helpless, those that are your own. She's a sinner, she knows, and proud, and angry at God to the point of hatred, but she knows she's made a fortress for her own and for whoever seeks shelter there, and it's good, worthy and priceless.

Lester asks why she stays in this tent, as though she knew the answer herself. What is it? The sound of Middle C ringing in her ears? The boy that doesn't know her? That big, old house that fights her? Or the voice of that house that sometimes whispers to her: wait, wait.

SCENE 64

House. DOLLY *waits.* SAM *walks in.*

DOLLY: Jesus, Sam, where have you been? What happened?

SAM: I tell you, Doll. It's been a bloody long haul. It was a bloody long night. I was desperate for a smoke but I didn't have time to bot one, I was concentratin' that hard. The only sober man there. Crikey, you're sober too.

DOLLY: What happened to you?!

SAM: I stayed in there the whole way.

DOLLY: And what happened? Fuckin' tell me!

SAM: Tell you? All right... I did it. I won the bank. The whole damn cake and candles. [*Pulling wads of money out of his pockets he calls over the fence.*] Lester?

LESTER *appears.* SAM *gives him money.* LESTER *stares at it, pockets it, goes inside.* DOLLY *opens her arms to him.*

DOLLY: Come here, you little stumpy bastard!

SCENE 65

TOBY *and* ROSE *lie together at the beach.*

TOBY: I dream about getting out of here. Out of Perth. Going to Bloomsbury or the Left Bank, or Sydney at a pinch.

ROSE: I'm happy here on Cottesloe Beach. I like it better than going to those fancy foreign joints. I spend all afternoon dressing up to impress your friends.

TOBY: You don't have to impress them!

ROSE: What about you?

TOBY: A man would have to be stupid not to think you're pretty. Whatever you wear.

He kisses her.

You know, we don't have to wear anything here. We could both...

He mimes dropping his daks.

ROSE: No, thank you, Toby Raven. I've read your poems. I must have typed twenty that were all about sex.

TOBY: You love it!

ROSE: Not when I'm typing.

TOBY: Just for that, you don't get your present.

ROSE: Please. Come on...

TOBY: If you tell a man he's obsessed with sex—

ROSE: I take it all back.

He hands her a plain-wrapped book.

Lady Chatterley's Lover! Where'd you get this!

TOBY: At the paper. Turn to page 190. Third paragraph.

ROSE: It falls open right there. [*She finds the paragraph.*] Crikey...

TOBY: Read it to me.

ROSE: Out loud?

He nods, grins.

I can't.

TOBY: Or we could take it back to my place and act out a few scenes. I could be the lusty gamekeeper and—

ROSE: Lusty? That'll be the day.

TOBY: Steady on! Read me some, then. I dare you.

ROSE: I dare you to come and get wet for once. Come on, time you learned to bodysurf.

TOBY: You want to be responsible for drowning one of this country's best unpublished poets?

ROSE: You wouldn't drown. I'd save you. Come on!

TOBY: You go. I'll watch you.

ROSE: No. You'll read that book and turn on your stomach to cover your stiffie. [*She heads towards the water.*] Rose really likes Toby Raven, loves him probably. He's different from the other blokes she meets, the ones with bad breath and Brylcreem in their hair. Most important though, Toby knows nothing about Cloudstreet. Out of shame, Rose never takes him there. They spend days in his flat as he dictates poems to her, poems that always get knocked back by one of the smart magazines over East. But at night she can't help telling him about her life in the old house, bit by bit she tells him. Then, lying beside him as he sleeps, she sees them married with a new house in the clean new suburbs, with all his clever friends dropping in to make her laugh. She wears a cashmere sweater tied loosely round her neck. Her hair's always wet and combed back after swimming. Her children have sweet faces, and they're adored by every passing stranger.

SCENE 66

Margaret River.

FRED: Fred tells no one that Quick was a Lamb. People round Margaret River still remember those Bible-bashers and their dud miracle. For a year, Quick drives for Fred. Quick does a good job with stiff steering and slack brakes and keeping wide of the transport coppers and their safety rules. He canes himself with work. Day and night, six days a week, he just drives. And on the seventh day, instead of resting, he cuts out bits from the newspaper and covers his caravan walls with pictures of sad bastards, unlucky bastards.

QUICK: One night, Quick loses his brakes on a hill before a rail crossing. Nine ton of super on the back and it isn't stopping. Quick goes down through the gears like a man down a fire escape. There's a train coming and he's going to hit it sure as shit. The handbrake is useless and all he has left is the ditch at the roadside. He spins the wheel and his tyres snick the rails and the train's on top of him and he hears an almighty crack like a neck breaking, and turns round to see his rear view mirror saluting him all the way down the tracks. The train punches past, an inch away, and he just makes it, but he bogs the truck beside the rails.

QUICK *is spattered with mud.*

FRED: Geez, look at you. You been sleepin' with the pigs?

QUICK: I just dug that bloody knocker out of the paddock. I want a couple of days off.

FRED: What for?

QUICK: Go fishin'. I nearly killed myself tonight.

FRED *is not impressed.*

I nearly lost the truck.

FRED: You should have. It's old, and it's insured.

QUICK: I nearly lost nine ton of super.

FRED: Take the week. Use my boat. I'll take it out of your pay.

QUICK *climbs into the boat and rows away.*

SCENE 67

In the boat QUICK *hears laughter and voices from the past.*

VOICES: Fish! Fish! Fish!

FISH'S VOICE: Boo!

Laughter.

LESTER'S VOICE: Come on, boys, let's get some tucker!

FISH'S VOICE: Oi, Quick, look at Dad.

Sounds swell as the memory washes over QUICK.

LESTER'S VOICE: Cheeky blighter! Don't smile too much, Fish, you'll frighten the prawns away.

The memory turns bad.

ORIEL'S VOICE: Do you see him?!

QUICK: No, I lost him!

LESTER'S VOICE: Fish!

QUICK: Just pull! Pull!

ORIEL'S VOICE: Oh Lord! No!

LESTER'S VOICE: Get the truck!

ORIEL'S VOICE: Blessed Saviour, bring him back! Jesus Almighty, raise him up! Now you, raise him up!

LESTER'S VOICE: Yes, Lord, yes!

ORIEL'S VOICE: Lord Jesus!

LESTER'S VOICE: He's alive!

ORIEL'S VOICE: It's a miracle!

ALL: Fish!! Fish!

> QUICK *fishes.*

BLACK MAN: Then it all begins. The first bite rings in his wrist like a cover drive. When he hauls the fish into the boat, it's two fishes, one fixed to the tail of the other. He baits up and casts again. He gets a strike the moment the hook hits the water. And then another, and another. He drags in four fish, two hooked and two biting their tails. He catches them cast after cast. His hands bleed and his arms ache and his boat vibrates like a cathedral with all these fish arching, beating and bucking.

Quick throws out baitless hooks to drag in great silver chains of them. They shine like money, and in the end he stops casting and lies back in the smother and squelch of fish as they leap in the boat of their own accord. He feels them slide across his chest as his head sinks into them, against his cheeks, along his lips with the briny taste of Lucy Wentworth's bits. He breathes them in and he looks up and sees the figure of a man walking upon the water. And it makes him laugh.

'He's on a sandbar,' thinks Quick. 'He must be. And he's black. But everyone's black at a distance.'

> *At the piano* FISH *cries, banging on Middle C, growing more discordant and guttural. The* GHOSTS *watch.*

FISH: Quick. Quick. Quick!

BLACK MAN: Then the black man picks him up and carries him towards shore. Glowing.

> *The* BLACK MAN *lifts* QUICK *from the sinking boat.*

76

SCENE 68

Cloudstreet, morning. On the LAMB *side,* FISH *laughs and dances around the house.* LESTER *pursues him, trying to get him dressed.* ELAINE *and* RED *get* HAT *into her wedding dress. On the* PICKLES *side,* SAM *makes breakfast,* DOLLY *sleeps and* ROSE *dresses for work.*

FISH: Quick! Quick!

LESTER: Fish, come and get dressed, son.

SAM: Rose! Brekky's ready.

HAT: If you hook me again I'm gonna knock your block into your frock, you hear me?

> ELAINE *bursts into tears.* LESTER *starts to dress* FISH, *who still laughs.*

ORIEL: Elaine! Settle down! You show some patience, Hat, or the whole cricket match'll be cancelled!

HAT: You can't!

ORIEL: We're paying for it if we're staying for it, so you button your lip and let your sisters dress you. You're not playing marbles now. This is a wedding for grown-ups. Any more griping and you're not invited.

HAT: But it's my wedding!

ORIEL: Bumslash! It's your marriage. The wedding belongs to us. Behave yourself.

> ROSE *joins* SAM. *They can hear the hubbub next door.*

HAT: Oh, Mum!

ORIEL: You look beautiful, now shut up!

ROSE: The sergeant major's at it again.

LESTER: Settle down, son. It's Hat's big day, Fishcake. She's gonna be married.

> *The* BLACK MAN *is approaching the house carrying the glowing* QUICK *in his arms.*

FISH: Quick.

LESTER: What?

FISH: Quick, Lestah.

LESTER: No, Geoffrey Birch, from Pemberton. He's a timber man.

> *The* BLACK MAN *knocks at the door.*

77

FISH: Quick.

LESTER: Oh, Gawd, there's someone at the door.

ORIEL: Who's that?

FISH: Quick.

LESTER: Someone get the door.

ORIEL: You get it, I've got the bucket.

> RED *and* ELAINE *head for the door.*

SAM: Let's hope it's not the groom.

> RED *and* ELAINE *open the door. The* BLACK MAN *has* QUICK
> *in his arms.* FISH *dances.*

BLACK MAN: Does this fella belong here?

RED / ELAINE: Mum? Dad? It's Quick! Is he all right?

BLACK MAN: He's all right, he's just a bit lost.

LESTER: Lord, he's glowin' like a lamp. Hala-bloody-lujah!

ORIEL: Get your mouth out of gear and help me get him inside.
You're a pimple of a man sometimes, Lester Lamb.

> *They carry* QUICK *into the house.*

RED / ELAINE: Lift! Lift! Lift!

LESTER: Oh, but you love me.

> *They take* QUICK *from the* BLACK MAN.

Come in. Make yourself at home.

BLACK MAN: No, I'll be moving on.

> *And he's gone.*

ORIEL: He's thin.

LESTER: He's home.

ORIEL: He looks terrible, and don't smarm.

> ROSE, *going out the front door, sees them with* QUICK.

ROSE: Good morning.

LESTER: Damn right.

HAT: That's it! That stabs that in the guts!

ORIEL: Leave off with the racket, Hat—

HAT: But it's my day, my wedding!

ORIEL: Go upstairs and make up your bed for him. You won't be
needing it.

> HAT *bursts into tears and goes, followed by* ELAINE *and* RED.

LESTER: Tell me you're happy. Tell me you're happy to have him back.

ORIEL: I'm happy. I'm happy, just lift your end. We've got a wedding on.

They put QUICK *to bed. The* LAMBS *leave. Bells toll.*

SCENE 69

As the bells fade QUICK *lies in bed asleep, glowing.* FISH *sits at the foot of his bed, guarding him from the* GHOSTS *of the house.*

FISH: Your light's goin', Quick. No more light soon. Good old Quick. Up soon. Then we'll go on the water.

Time passes. FISH *leaves the foot of* QUICK'*s bed.*

SCENE 70

ORIEL *sits on the bed.* QUICK *stirs.*

QUICK: G'day.

ORIEL: Hello.

QUICK: I thought you wouldn't speak to me.

ORIEL: A woman don't need talk. She needs a team. I'm your mother, you know.

QUICK: Geez, how could I forget?

ORIEL: Not by runnin' away.

QUICK: I feel like Rip Van Winkle. Do we fly to the moon yet?

ORIEL: Only on the wireless. What did you see?

QUICK: What do you mean?

ORIEL: When you were away. You saw something.

QUICK: I don't know.

ORIEL: I'm your mother.

QUICK: I don't know, I said.

ORIEL: You broke Fish's heart, Quick. People aren't like furniture. He sat on your bed holding you when you were sleeping, kind of expecting you to float away again. I'm sorry, I didn't want to go crook... What did you see, Quick?

QUICK: Why are you living in that tent?

ORIEL: I asked you first.

79

QUICK: What's for brekky?

ORIEL: Quick.

He looks away.

QUICK: I saw myself runnin', that's all. In the wheat fields. I saw myself runnin'.

ORIEL: Well, that's enough, I suppose.

QUICK: You bet.

Beat.

ORIEL: Do you still blame yourself for it?

QUICK: For what?

ORIEL: Fish.

QUICK: How did you know about that?

ORIEL: I'm your mother. Besides, it's obvious. Fish was everyone's favourite. People say they don't have them, but that's a lie we tell to protect the others.

QUICK: You loved him more than the rest of us?

ORIEL: Wasn't he your favourite, Quick? Didn't you love him more than all of us? Don't you still love him more?

QUICK: What would you know? You don't know the first thing about feelings, certainly not mine, damn sure not what I feel about Fish.

ORIEL: You think it's your fault. You think it should have been you. And you don't realise that's rubbish.

QUICK: You don't know a damn thing about it, Mum.

ORIEL: Have I been a crook mother?

QUICK: No, of course not.

ORIEL: Do I lie?

QUICK: No.

ORIEL: Do I cheat?

QUICK: No.

ORIEL: Steal?

QUICK: No.

ORIEL: Fornicate?

QUICK: Well, I'll have to check on that with the neighbours. I reckon that tent's a dubious sign.

ORIEL: Don't be a drongo, Quick. What's wrong with me?

QUICK: Mum.

ORIEL: Come on, what's my problem?

QUICK: I've never known you to be like this. It's like having a dead shark in the boat. Those buggers have a habit of coming to life and taking your foot off.

ORIEL: I don't want your foot. What's my problem, son?

QUICK: You don't have enough fun, maybe.

ORIEL: No one asks me to dance anymore. I used to dance with my daughters until I lost out to men, and Heaven knows I dance better than any of them.

QUICK: Let's face it, Mum, you do everythin' better than anybody.

ORIEL: I'm glad you see things my way. The strong are here to look after the weak, son, and the weak are here to teach the strong.

QUICK: What are we here to teach you, Mum?

ORIEL: Too early to say.

SCENE 71

Lamb kitchen. Morning. LESTER *makes breakfast.* FISH *spins bowls or plates on the table.*

LON: Keep it down.

FISH: They're up. I keep them up.

LON: Brilliant, just flamin' brilliant, Fish.

LESTER: Cut your grizzlin', Lon, you'll be late for work.

LON: I'm waitin' for my eggs.

LESTER: You'll be wearin' 'em if you don't shut up.

FISH whoops. The plates clatter.

LON: Jesus, Fish!

LESTER seizes LON by the ear.

LESTER: If your mother was here she'd wash your mouth out, boy. It'd be Trusol paste at least. Don't let me hear you talk like that again.

He lets go.

LON: He makes a racket!

LESTER: Can't you cope with him havin' a bit of fun? His prospects aren't as brilliant as yours, you know. Ever thought about that? If you can't show him any respect—

LON: Respect! He's a Clydesdale. A retard! He should be put away.

LESTER *comes at* LON, *who backs away.*

FISH: Don't hit us! Lestah, don't hit us!

LON *tries to bolt but* ORIEL *appears in the doorway.*

ORIEL: What's this?

LESTER: I've never had any cause to feel ashamed of a child of mine.

ORIEL: The eggs are burning, Lester.

LESTER: Yes, I know, woman, I know.

QUICK *appears behind* ORIEL.

Mornin', Quick. Welcome home.

FISH: He's gone out. His light's off.

LON: I'm goin'.

LESTER: Take a wrench to your neck, son, and get your head off and see if you can't give it a good flush out. A plumber should always mind his own blockages.

LON *goes.*

QUICK: He's a plumber?

ORIEL: Apprentice.

FISH: You been gone a hundred, Quick.

QUICK: Yeah. You've got big, too.

LESTER *serves him a plate of eggs.*

LESTER: It's hardly the fatted calf.

ELAINE *and* RED *come in.*

ELAINE: Hello, stranger.

QUICK: God, look at these two!

RED: Where you been, you slack bludger?

QUICK: Red, you've grown up.

RED: Glad you still know my name. I'll have my nursing certificate next year.

QUICK: How about you, Elaine? What you up to?

ELAINE: Still working for Mum. I'm engaged.

RED: Waiting for him to pop the question. Been waiting for years.

ELAINE: Shut up, Red! Roger's just a bit shy.

LESTER: There's porridge.

ELAINE: There's always porridge.
ORIEL: Be grateful there's food on the table.
LESTER: Your mother's not well. She's havin' an attack of smiles.
ORIEL: Don't stand about, Elaine. That shop won't open up by itself.

SCENE 72

ROSE *types a poem.* TOBY *stands behind her.*

TOBY: What do you think?
ROSE: It's good.
TOBY: Really?
ROSE: Yes, of course. It's good. *Parthenos.* What's that?
TOBY: Virgin. As in the Parthenon.
ROSE: Oh. And *gymnastikos*?
TOBY: Athletic. Don't you like it?
ROSE: Yes. I just don't understand all of it.

> TOBY *scowls.*

Please don't do that.
TOBY: What?
ROSE: Scowl at everything I say.
TOBY: I don't.
ROSE: You do. Specially round your friends.
TOBY: Well, Rose, sometimes you do stop things dead.
ROSE: At least I don't speak with my head back and my eyes closed
with those fake Pommy accents.
TOBY: You just don't understand them, Rose.
ROSE: I understand them, mate. Just like I understand your poems,
which I've been typing every weekend for months.

> *She starts to leave.*

TOBY: So you don't like them.
ROSE: I like them, I like them!
TOBY: Tell me the truth.
ROSE: Toby...
TOBY: The truth. Please.

> ROSE *stares at him. Silence.*

ROSE: Sorry, mate, I'm not a typist. And I don't think you're a poet.

TOBY: You want to marry me, don't you?

ROSE: You said it yourself. Ambition, Toby, it twists us into funny shapes. Please, let's forget all this, eh? I just want to be with you. Let's go somewhere where we don't have to be with seventeen of your smart friends. Let's go to the footie tomorrow. Stuff the poetry.

> TOBY *laughs.*

It was just an idea.

TOBY: An idea!

ROSE: Yes, the switchgirl gets an idea. Call me a taxi.

TOBY: I'll call you a lot of things.

ROSE: I'm going home.

TOBY: Ah, the mysterious home. I'd love to see where all those Gothic strains come from.

> ROSE *leaves.*

SCENE 73

By the water. Night. QUICK *has a fishing net.*

QUICK: Quick finds an old boat on the bank at Crawley, the one he and Fish rowed from Fremantle, still sitting where they left it.

> LESTER *watches.*

I'm going to put this to work, Dad, earn my keep. You can sell what I catch.

LESTER: You'd be wastin' your brains here on the river, son. You need some ambition.

QUICK: What ambition did you have?

LESTER: When I was a kid I wanted to be a hero. Then I wanted to be loved. Now I'll settle for being a good man.

QUICK: That's all I want.

LESTER: Easy to be a good man out on the water. There's no one else to think of. But here, where all the lights are, where all the people are, that's the test.

> LESTER *goes.*

QUICK: Quick rows down the narrows and puts out lines for mulloway, flathead and bream. On clear nights he can see lights in the hills and the scarp beyond the city. He remembers the wheatbelt, that great riverless domain, recalls himself charging madly through the wheat, and realises he was looking for this, for the river. Every important thing that ever happened to him had to do with a river. Sometimes he thinks it's the land's blood. Other times he thinks it's the sewer. But the water makes him happy, lets him think.

FISH *watches.*

Quick feels like his own boss again. Oriel sells his catch. The shop prospers. And Fish starts coming out of his room in the afternoons to watch his brother mend the nets.

FISH: Can I come, Quick?

QUICK: Not tonight, no.

FISH: Please.

QUICK: Sorry, mate.

He leaves the house.

Quick likes to be on the water, he has plenty of time out there to think alone. But he knows he's putting something off.

SCENE 74

TOBY RAVEN *arrives at Cloudstreet. He sees* FISH.

TOBY: Have I got the Pickles house?

FISH: Lester sells pickles. In the shop.

TOBY: The Pickles family.

FISH: Pickles family. Mister Pickles! Missus Pickles! Ted Pickles, Rose Pickles and Fatty Chub Pickles.

SAM *comes out.*

TOBY: I was looking for Rose Pickles. I'm Toby Raven.

SAM: Come on in. Rose. Rose! There's a bloke here!

ROSE: Who?

SAM: Says his name's Tony.

ROSE *appears.*

ROSE: What the hell are you doing here?

TOBY: Someone's taken one of my poems.

SAM: Hope you're insured. I'll bung the kettle on.

TOBY: It's going to be published in *Westerly*. And I'm on the short list for the State Poetry Prize. They're announcing it tonight, and we're invited.

SAM: All of us?

ROSE: Put the bloody kettle on, Dad.

> SAM *goes.*

How did you find us?

TOBY: The girls on the switch. They remembered the street. Once I found that, it was easy. Everybody knows this place. Come on, Rose, don't be dark on me.

ROSE: Congratulations on the poem.

TOBY: You're not the same girl I heard on the switch last year.

ROSE: No, I know about Earl Grey tea now and I've read Rimbaud and his imitators.

TOBY: Nasty, nasty.

ROSE: Don't you bloody patronise me.

TOBY: Jesus, Rose, it's my big day. I'm asking you out to a do. I've cracked it at last. They're welcoming us in.

ROSE: The establishment? I thought you were avant-garde or whatever.

TOBY: Come on, be nice.

ROSE: Nice is a terrible bourgeois word.

TOBY: You're a sharp girl, Rose.

ROSE: And I type like a demon.

TOBY: Come on, I wanted you to be the first to hear. Even if you don't like the stuff, I thought you'd be pleased that someone else does. Come with me tonight. We'll drink champagne and look interesting.

ROSE: I don't know, Toby…

TOBY: Please. I'm sorry for barging in on your hideaway.

> *He points to* FISH, *who watches them.*

Is that the boy? The one you…

> *She shooshes him sharply.*

Please come with me tonight.

Beat. She nods.

I'll pick you up at eight. Look pretty for me. You could be my good luck charm.

He goes.

SCENE 75

Night. QUICK *packs fishing gear.*

FISH: Can I come, Quick?
QUICK: Not tonight, no.
FISH: When? How many sleeps?
QUICK: Mum says no, Fish. She doesn't want you goin' on the river.
FISH: I like it.
QUICK: Yeah, I know, cobber.
FISH: But I'm big!
QUICK: Yeah, that's true enough, I reckon.
FISH: Carn.
QUICK: Carn what?
FISH: Carn, take me. You did once. You took me one time. Remember? We goed in the stars.
QUICK: We were kids, Fish. We were asleep. It was a dream.
FISH: We saw.
QUICK: Nah.
FISH: You're lying. [*Beat.*] Please.
QUICK: All right. Come on.

SCENE 76

ROSE *and* TOBY *are at a literary reception.* GUESTS *chat and drink and mostly ignore them.* MEREDITH *passes.*

MEREDITH: Toby! Fingers crossed. Hello, Rose. Isn't it nerve-racking?

HEADLEY, *the editor, claps his hands.*

HEADLEY: Ladies and gentlemen, we shan't keep you in suspense any longer. We had a strong field of entrants this year, and from them we drew a short list of highly individual and promising

87

young poets. The other judges and I have conferred and you'll be pleased to know our view was unanimous. The State Poetry Prize, this handsome medallion, together with a cheque for a hundred guineas and a year's subscription to our magazine, goes to Anthea Bradley. Anthea?

Applause. ANTHEA *steps forward.* TOBY *takes another drink.*

ROSE: Don't worry, there's always next year.

TOBY: Thanks.

MEREDITH: Sorry.

TOBY: What does it matter? After all, Perth is the biggest country town in the world trying to be a city.

MEREDITH: The most isolated country town in the world…

TOBY: Trying desperately to hit the big time.

ROSE *is apart from* TOBY *and near* ANTHEA *in the crush.*

ROSE: Congratulations.

ANTHEA: Thanks. I'm sorry, I don't [know your name]…?

ROSE: I'm Rose. I'm not a writer. I came with Toby.

ANTHEA: Toby?

ROSE: Toby Raven. He was on the short list.

ANTHEA: Toby Raven. I haven't read any of his work.

ROSE: I have. All of it. I've typed every word. He's good.

ANTHEA: Lucky man. He has a secretary.

She goes as other GUESTS *congratulate her.* ROSE *sees* TOBY *with* MEREDITH *and her* PARTNER. *He can't see* ROSE.

TOBY: Shoot me down for heresy, but poetry might have had its day. Fiction now… This town is full of fodder for a really good comic novel. It's fabulously absurd. There's a great big tumbledown old ruin…

He sees ROSE. *A beat, then he goes on.*

Rose knows all about it. She grew up there.

MEREDITH: Oh, tell all.

TOBY: Yes, tell them.

ROSE: About what?

TOBY: About your father's stump, and his job at the Mint. The lady in the tent. And the slow boy you used to love.

ROSE *stares at* TOBY.

It could be brilliant. A kind of grotesquerie. I've always thought so. Tell them, Rose. Tell them! Rose!

ROSE *runs out.*

SCENE 77

QUICK *and* FISH *are on the river in the boat.*

QUICK: You hungry? There's some pies in the box. Where's your beanie?

FISH: In my pocket.

QUICK: Put it on, it's cold.

FISH: Don't boss!

QUICK: Who brought you out in this boat? Whose boat is it?

FISH: It's our boat, all of us. I remember.

QUICK: Come on, let's have something to eat. The cobblers can wait.

FISH: Not lookin' at them.

QUICK: Just the water, eh?

FISH: Yep.

QUICK: You're a character, all right. What are we gonna do with ourselves, Fish?

FISH: Eat pies more. You sleep. I'll watch.

QUICK: You happy?

FISH: I get happy sometimes. Not you.

QUICK: Oh, me, I'm the original glumbum.

FISH: I like the water.

QUICK: You remember what happened to you in the water, at Margaret? When we were little?

FISH: Is it a story?

QUICK: It happened, but it can be a story.

FISH: I know a story. The house hurts, you know.

QUICK: What's that?

FISH: A story.

ROSE *is crying in the shadows on the bank.*

QUICK: There's someone on the bank there.

FISH: Some people cry.

QUICK: Shut up, Fish, someone is crying.

FISH: In the story, Quick—

QUICK: Shut up and stay down! [*He rows towards the shore, holds up a lamp.*] Is everything all right there? Sorry, I didn't mean—

ROSE: Is that Quick Lamb? Quick and Fish. Well, fancy this. You don't remember me.

FISH: It's Rose.

QUICK: From next door?

FISH: She's not happy, Quick.

ROSE: Any chance of a ride?

QUICK: Where?

ROSE: It doesn't matter.

QUICK: Here, hop in.

> *She gets in.*

FISH: Tickets, please.

> ROSE *laughs, then starts to cry.* FISH *lies in her lap and falls asleep.* ROSE *recovers.*

QUICK: Want a fag?

ROSE: Thanks, I don't smoke.

QUICK: Fair enough.

ROSE: He's asleep.

QUICK: There's some Chateau Tanunda in that coat, if you want a swig.

ROSE: No, it's all right.

QUICK: No smokin' and no drinkin'. Do your parents know about this?

ROSE: Suppose it is a bit of a laugh, really.

QUICK: Think I'll take a snort myself. Could you find it?

ROSE: Actually, I might have a swig after all that.

> *She swigs, coughs and splutters.*

QUICK: Well, that's cheered you up.

ROSE: It's beautiful out here. Your brother... What's the story with him?

> *He sighs.*

Sorry. But your mob and mine never really talked much, did they? I'm sorry.

QUICK: Doesn't matter. He's been after me forever about coming. Mum and Dad worry. I smuggled him out. He's knackered.

ROSE: What are you like, Quick Lamb?

QUICK: What sort of question's that?

ROSE: Can't you answer it?

QUICK: What am I like? A bit lost, I suppose.

ROSE: The lost Lamb.

QUICK: Yeah, I feel a bit sheepish about that.

ROSE: We should get our own show on the wireless.

QUICK: God, you're smilin'.

ROSE: No, it's only a rumour. Well, what are you like? We live at the same house for years, and I don't even know who you are. I remember that time you clobbered me on the stairs with a bag. Knocked me down, you rotten sod. You remember that?

QUICK: No. Don't think so.

ROSE: Well, you were in a hurry.

QUICK: You grew up pretty good lookin', Rose.

ROSE: Ta. How come you do this?

QUICK: Fishin'? It's pleasant enough and pays my way. I haven't got any ideas about what to do. My old man was restless, goin' from thing to thing. Suppose that means we're weak.

ROSE: What do you think about all day?

QUICK: I reckon I'm tryin' to figure out what I lost. I keep figurin' I've lost something somewhere.

ROSE: Something to do with him?

QUICK: I reckon my whole life is to do with him.

ROSE: You really love him, don't you?

QUICK: Everyone loved him. He was the funniest, stupidest kid in the whole bloody world, and everybody loved him. He's my brother.

ROSE: Geez, I've got two of them, and I couldn't say I even liked them.

QUICK: You would have loved him.

ROSE: I probably did.

She strokes the sleeping FISH.

You reckon we'd be any good married to each other?

QUICK: Gimme that bottle!

91

He hurls the bottle into the water.

ROSE: What'd you do that for?

QUICK: Reckon you've had enough.

ROSE: I'm still pretty bloody sober, thank you very much. And it was just a question, you know. Hypothetical, as the smartbums say.

QUICK: You've been around with smartbums. I wouldn't know.

ROSE: Fair enough.

QUICK: Yeah.

ROSE: You're true blue, Quick Lamb. Now answer the question.

They've rowed home. FISH *stays asleep in the boat.*

SCENE 78

Cloudstreet. ROSE *and* QUICK *pass through the silent house. They reach the windowless room. The* OLD WOMAN *and the* BLACK GIRL *stir.*

BLACK MAN: Rose and Quick burst into the windowless room while the rest of the house sleeps.

QUICK: They could be children, they breathe so hard, standing apart from one another lit only by the glow of their faces and the heat of their breaths.

ROSE: I just stumbled into Heaven. You believe in fate?

He shakes his head.

This isn't happening.

QUICK: Not yet.

ROSE: I know you all of a sudden.

QUICK: We're nuts. We're gunna be embarrassed afterwards.

ROSE: No, we're gunna be something else altogether. Come here, Quick Lamb.

BLACK MAN: Then suddenly they're going off like a bag of penny bombs, clawing at each other's clothes, talking into skin and opening up. Rose's shoulders slope sweetly under Quick's hands and she presses into his belly, finds his nipples at her fingertips as she takes him down to the faded flowers of the library rug. The girlshadow and the hagshadow go limp and open-mouthed. They see the living find curves and dips in one another and hear electric whispers building in their space. They're pressed against the walls, and it's love pressing them, see how it distorts their meatless shadows. Rose wraps Quick in her legs, knots over him with hands and mouth and hair, while Quick sprinkles her with sweat, shaking as he is. Across the knots of their discarded clothes they slide and clinch, he with fishblood and her blood on his fingers, she with brandy on her breath, and together they make a balloon of heat inside the cold nausea of that dead room whose timbers twist and creak; a new dwelling place. After they've dressed and gone, hurrying out into the daylit house with news for the world, their sudden love remains in the room, hanging like incense.

SCENE 79

Next morning. QUICK *finds* ORIEL, ROSE *finds* SAM.

QUICK: It's probably a bit of a shock, Mum.

SAM *laughs in the Pickles kitchen.*

ORIEL: Well, I see Mr Pickles has been informed.

LESTER *emerges from the house.*

LESTER: You've left the fish out, son. The cats are getting to it.

QUICK: I'm getting married, Dad. I'm marrying Rose next door.

LESTER: Good God. She's so pretty.

RED *and* ELAINE *emerge.*

RED: Good on you, Quick. I knew you weren't completely useless. You don't deserve her.

ELAINE: But I'm the one that's engaged!

DOLLY *and* SAM *are in the Pickles kitchen.*

SAM: Well, it's a step down from Tony from the uni, but he seems a good boy.

DOLLY: That's all he is. A good boy. You up the duff?

ROSE: Leave it out, Mum!

DOLLY: Them Lambs'll hate it.

ROSE: You mean you hate it.

DOLLY: That woman'll tear you to bits.

CHUB *comes in.*

CHUB: What's all the yellin'?

SAM: She's gettin' married to Quick Lamb in six weeks.

CHUB: Oh. There any bacon?

DOLLY: She wants our blessing, but she won't ask for it.

ROSE: What do you reckon, Dad?

SAM: Oh, you know me, I'll always back an outside chance. He'll have to come and see me.

ROSE: He'll come.

SAM: We'll get free fish, I suppose.

ROSE: I reckon it could be arranged.

DOLLY: They're gettin' this place off us, bit by bit. We're signin' ourselves over.

SAM: It'll be a bloody dry wedding.

DOLLY: Not if we're payin' for it. No flamin' fear!

> *The house is set up for a wedding breakfast.* HAT *and* GEOFF BIRCH *arrive. A bridal waltz starts.* ROSE *and* QUICK *step out.*

ROSE: I want to live in a new house.

QUICK: We've got no money.

ROSE: I've been working for years. I've been saving all this time.

QUICK: I haven't even got a job. Mum never pays me for the fish.

ROSE: We'll see her about that tomorrow. Don't be gutless, Quick. You should've been paid.

QUICK: I need a job. Two jobs if we're supposed to have a house.

ROSE: We'll get you two jobs.

QUICK: You'll be quittin', I suppose.

ROSE: No, Quick, I won't be quitting.

QUICK: I thought girls like to.

ROSE: Not this girl. This girl wants to buy a house. When we get back from the honeymoon we're going to State Housing to sign up. What'll you do?

QUICK: For a job? Join the police force.

ROSE: God, why?

QUICK: Don't you read the paper?

ROSE: Of course I read the bloody paper.

QUICK: Evil.

ROSE: What?

QUICK: I want to fight evil.

ROSE: You're not in a comic, Quick.

QUICK: Why'd everyone leave it so late to tell me?

> ROSE *dances with* SAM. QUICK *asks* ORIEL *for a dance. She gets up, but crosses the floor and asks* DOLLY *to dance.* DOLLY *puts out her cigarette and rises.* ORIEL *steers* DOLLY *round the floor. All watch. Then all dance out.* FISH *sleeps, watched by the* BLACK MAN.

END OF PART TWO

PART THREE

SCENE 80

The GHOSTS *swirl about Cloudstreet. The* COMPANY *cross the stage accompanying three screams:* DOLLY; ROSE; *and a* VICTIM *murdered by the* NEDLANDS MONSTER *who is seen in shadow as he kills.*

DOLLY: Teddy! He was the one I loved. He was the one! You can all go and fuckin' die because I want him back! He was the one!

> ROSE *is on her hands and knees, clutching her stomach.*

ROSE: Call someone! Call someone, Quick! I'm losing the baby!

> *The* NEDLANDS MONSTER *can still be seen in shadow.* FISH *bangs on the piano in the windowless room.*

BLACK MAN: There's evil in the air. Ted Pickles dies of a heart attack in Adelaide. Rose miscarries her baby at four months. And in the streets of Perth, a little man discovers what rape and murder mean. There's a woman. Young. Her short nightie rucked up in the heat. The little man finds the cord from the bedlight. It's so easy. The whole city starts to quake in fear at the thought of him.

> *The* MONSTER *vanishes.*

FISH: No... No... No! I hate youse, you stupids! This is my house!

> SAM *finds* FISH *moaning. The* GHOSTS *dance.*

They won't let me play!

SAM: I know how it feels, son.

> FISH *moans and thumps the walls louder.*

Hello? Is there someone up?

> ELAINE *comes sleepily into the room.*

ELAINE: Mr Pickles?

SAM: Do you feel it? I thought I was having a heart attack.

ELAINE: What? What's happening?

SAM: It's the Shifty Shadow. I haven't felt it like this since I lost...
[my fingers]

ELAINE: Where's his clothes?

FISH: They won't let me play.

SCENE 81

BLACK MAN: Yes, there's a killer out there, slinking along, in your
town, in your yard, in your street and hating you, every whole
one of you, as you sleep. Coming for you. Wherever the hot
desert wind blows him. West Perth, Dalkeith, Shenton Park,
Subiaco... He's coming for you. For all of you.

QUICK, *in uniform, is at Nedlands Police Station with* SARGE,
his boss.

QUICK: You gotta let me go out. I'm doing nothing here, Sarge.

SARGE: You're manning the desk. That's your job for now.

QUICK: Just one patrol. Please. I'll work a double. You don't even
have to pay me.

SARGE: Lamb, this is not your problem.

QUICK: Three people have been murdered.

SARGE: In another suburb. That's someone else's problem. Not ours.

QUICK: There's evil out there, Sarge.

SARGE: Not in Nedlands. We're a blue-ribbon station. We show the
colours and hear the complaints of the high and mighty.

QUICK: But we gotta do something!

SARGE: Why don't you start by making a cuppa while I have a kip in
one of the cells?

QUICK: Sarge—

The MONSTER*'s shadow slinks through the darkness.*

BLACK MAN: But the little man with the harelip kills again. This
time in Nedlands. Then a fifth time and everything goes still,
quaking at the thought of him. This is Perth, whose ambition
knows no bounds, and yet the streets are empty. It's sweltering,
but everyone keeps their doors and windows locked. Don't come

calling, they say. Ring three times. Don't go out. And no one does. Except Quick Lamb.

QUICK, *on patrol, moves through the dark.*

Armed with his handcuffs, torch and truncheon, he gets his patrol. Quick wants to see what evil really looks like, see whether it can be stopped. He can smell fear in every lane. There's someone out there killing and doing evil and he's losing the fight.

SCENE 82

ROSE *sits in a spotless caravan beside the new home-site.* SAM *enters with roses.*

ROSE: This is a surprise. Shouldn't you be at the races?
SAM: Well, shouldn't you be out doin' something?

ROSE *shrugs. He hands her the flowers.*

You look awful.
ROSE: Thanks. You'll want a cuppa.
SAM: Yeah. No milk.
ROSE: I remember, Dad. I'm the daughter, remember.
SAM: Yeah, I recall right enough. Small here, isn't it?
ROSE: New house won't be ready for a few months. Sorry it's such a mess.
SAM: A mess? Rosie, I could eat off the floor.
ROSE: You wouldn't know. You live at Cloudstreet. [*Beat.*] There must be something wrong.
SAM: I'm here about your mum.
ROSE: Can't manage a friendly visit?
SAM: We don't exactly see you makin' a nuisance of yourself visitin' Cloudstreet. Besides, it'd be a brave bastard who tried makin' a friendly visit on you.
ROSE: Let's just have a cuppa, shall we?
SAM: Ever since Ted died, your mum's been losin' control altogether.
ROSE: She never had any. Rats have more control than old Dolly.
SAM: Jesus, Rose. She's gettin' old and scared. If she doesn't lay off the slops a bit she'll die.

98

ROSE: You'd be better off moving out and leaving her to it. She'll never change, Dad. And you'll never change her.

SAM: Do you remember when you were a girl, you found me in the bathroom getting ready to slit my throat? You remember? You came in. I stopped. For you. She'll stop for you, too, you know.

ROSE: Dad, I cleaned up her vomit, washed her clothes, dragged her home from the pub every bloody night of my childhood. I did her work. I think I've done enough in that department.

SAM: She hasn't been able to get out of bed. She's grievin'. Ted was her favourite.

ROSE: You don't have to tell me! She only ever loved one of us.

SAM: For Christ's sake, how do you think that makes me feel? Show some pity, Rose. She lost a child.

ROSE: She's not the only one. I lost my baby and she hasn't come to see me once.

SAM: You never knew yours. It's not the same. She was Ted's mother.

ROSE: She was never a mother.

SAM: Don't be cruel to her, Rose. She's had her chances and she's nearly finished. Winnin' over someone like that isn't much of a victory. She can only lose from now on in. She can only get old and die. You're young. You can have more babies, things are ahead of you. Look at me. Whatever I'm gunna get I've had, and damn near all that's been lost. You can bear it when you lose money and furniture. You can take it when you lose your looks, your teeth, your youth. But, Christ Jesus, when your family goes, it's more than a man can handle.

SAM *goes.*

SCENE 83

The ghost of TED *passes as* DOLLY *thrashes in her bed.*

DOLLY: Teddy? Where are you goin' Teddy?

TED: Down the jetty, Mum, I'm gunna chuck a few bombies, I'm gunna stick a jellyfish down Rose's bathers.... .

DOLLY: Ted? Teddy? Don't leave me...

TED*'s ghost fades as* ROSE *approaches* DOLLY.

Teddy?

ROSE: No, it's me, Mum. Dad said you wanted to see me.

DOLLY: I'm tired.

ROSE: Well, I'm tired, too, so get on with it.

DOLLY: Don't hate me.

ROSE: Too late for that.

DOLLY: Why?

ROSE: My whole life, Mother, that's why.

DOLLY: What did I do that was so bad?

ROSE: You stole from me. My childhood, my trust, everything. You were a hateful bitch. A drunken slut. I hate you for all the reasons you hate yourself.

DOLLY: You look sick.

ROSE: What is all this anyway? Why the summons?

DOLLY: I was sad.

ROSE: About Ted? Your favourite.

DOLLY: People have them, Rose. You always loved Sam more than me.

ROSE: He earned it.

DOLLY: People don't earn it.

ROSE: They do with me. I'm going. This makes me want to vomit.

DOLLY: Everything makes you want to... Please, don't go. I want to talk, just to talk.

ROSE: I'm busy.

DOLLY: Please.

> ROSE *leaves. She finds* LESTER *outside, listening.*

ROSE: The old walls still have ears, eh?

LESTER: Please stay, love.

ROSE: No one should make me do this again. You don't know what this is like. Why should I stay?

LESTER: I dunno. I can't stand the hate. It'll kill you. You're one of us now and I couldn't bear to lose you. She's hurtin'. We all are. Please, Rose.

> *He leaves her.* ROSE *stands alone.*

ROSE: They're fucking, in there behind the door. Listen to them in there, snorting and—But Rose is a girl. She doesn't know what they're... Mum? There's been an accident. Dad's lost his fingers. And Dolly's in there with someone else. Rose's mother is on top of some stranger and Rose turns to steel right there.

ROSE *walks back into* DOLLY's *room.*

Better?

DOLLY: Feel like shit, but I reckon that's better. You look like you should sit down.

ROSE: I'm all right.

DOLLY: Sit down before you fall down. When are you gettin' pregnant again?

ROSE: I'm not thinking about it. Why do you ask?

DOLLY: I was plannin' on bein' a grandmother. This mornin'. That's when I decided. Be good for me, you know. I'd spoil them rotten. I'd give them lollies and fizzy drinks, let them wreck the bloody place. Reckon I'd be the worst bloody grandma a kid could have.

ROSE: Why not? You were already the worst mother.

DOLLY: They'd love me. I'd let them swear their heads off, give them noisy toys, take them to the pictures and stuff them with fairy floss. I wouldn't make them wear clothes. I wouldn't make them do anything, as long as they came to see me.

ROSE: You're a grandmother already. What about Ted's kid?

DOLLY: He's a thousand miles away. Don't know anything about him.

ROSE: Well, one day, maybe.

DOLLY: Oh yeah, Ted's wife is gonna get on a train and come and see Grandma Dolly.

ROSE: She's got the money. Ted was a good jockey. He rode winners.

DOLLY: Imagine being around a man who rode winners...

ROSE: It killed him, Dolly, trying to get his weight down one last time. They reckon his heart just stopped.

DOLLY: You reckon you'd have missed him more if he'd been a sister?

ROSE: What kind of a question's that? I never had a sister.

DOLLY: You wanted one, though, eh?

ROSE: I used to watch those Lamb girls and think of the things they could tell each other.

DOLLY: Sisters always look better from a distance. I had seven. Jesus, women together! You found out what a mother's like. You won't forget me in a hurry. Don't go moanin' about sisters.

ROSE: What was your mother like?

DOLLY: You should never trust a woman.

ROSE: I thought it was men you hated.

DOLLY: No, men are lovely. I was mad about men all my life.

ROSE: Yes.

DOLLY: It's women I hate.

ROSE: Daughters.

DOLLY: No, daughters are different. It's sisters I hate most. You should be grateful you never had any.

ROSE: I don't get it, Mum.

DOLLY: My sister...

ROSE: What?

DOLLY: My second oldest sister, the one who made me feel like rubbish all my life, she was my mother. There we were. There we were.

ROSE: My God. Mum! Oh, Mum. You never told me. You never ever said. Don't cry. Mum. Please.

> *But she starts to cry first. Mother and daughter hold each other.*

SCENE 84

QUICK, *on patrol, meets the* BLACK MAN.

QUICK: Haven't you got a home to go to?

BLACK MAN: Not this side of the river.

QUICK: Are you real?

BLACK MAN: Are you? *You've* got a home to go to, Quick. Go there. Go there.

SCENE 85

Cloudstreet. RED *comes home in a nurse's uniform.*

RED: I had to shave two blokes today before they went into theatre. Shave 'em all over.

ELAINE: Red...

RED: Geez, I hate men's bits. They—

ELAINE: Stop it!

RED: Elaine, it's better to be disgusted than ignorant. Now did you
    know that when they get excited—?
ELAINE: I don't want to know. I don't need to know anything.
RED: You will if Roger the dodger ever pops the question.
ELAINE: Roger's just shy!
RED: Crikey, will you look at Lon!

    LON *comes in with a black eye.* ORIEL *sees him.*

ORIEL: What bully did this to you?
LON: A man. A full-growed man.
ORIEL: I'll get you some ice for that. Come on. What did he do?
LON: He hit me.
ORIEL: Did you deserve some punishment? Lon?

    LON *opens the fridge door.*

  Answer me, son.
LON: There's a girl pregnant.
ORIEL: What?
LON: There's a girl pregnant.

    ORIEL *jams his head in the fridge door.*

  Owww! Mum, cut it out!

    LESTER *comes in.*

RED: It's Pansy Mullet, isn't it? Poor little cow.
LESTER: Leave off, Orry.
RED: Lucky it's only his head in there. If it was up to me, he'd be
    losin' his play bits.
ORIEL: You'll marry her, of course. And you'll bring her to live here.
LON: No friggin' way. Ow!

    ORIEL *presses harder on his head.*

  Ow!

SCENE 86

QUICK *hurries back to* ROSE *at the caravan.*

QUICK: I've had an idea.
ROSE: Watch yourself.
QUICK: More of a proposition really.

ROSE: Out with it.

QUICK: You haven't been sleeping well.

ROSE: I'm all right.

QUICK: And I'm working patrol most nights now.

ROSE: Yeah, that's what you wanted.

QUICK: And there's a murderer out there. If we go back to Cloudstreet—

ROSE: Quick—

QUICK: Just for a little while, till the house is finished. At least till we catch this bloke.

ROSE: No.

QUICK: Rose—

ROSE: No!

QUICK: Rosie, I'm worried about you here with no one to look out for you.

ROSE: Cloudstreet's too old, Quick. I hate old.

QUICK: I know, but—

ROSE: I want a clean, neat, new house that only we live in. I want a car out front and a mowed lawn—

QUICK: But just for—

ROSE: Clean and new, that's what I want for us and our baby.

QUICK: A couple of months till—What? What did you say?

ROSE: Don't faint on me, Casanova. You've done your job. I think I'm pregnant. I wasn't going to tell you till I felt pretty certain this one would stick.

QUICK: Rosie, are you sure?

ROSE: Yeah.

QUICK: Well, this is all the more reason to—

ROSE: No, listen to me. What'll happen if we go back to Cloudstreet? I'll tell you. Oriel will order me around and Dolly will want to be my new best friend. I've made my peace with her, but I don't want to live with her again. And Fish will want to sleep with us.

QUICK: No, he won't.

ROSE: Every night. I lived in the same house with you all your life, don't forget. I know what goes on on your side, mate. You can go back there if you want. Me and the baby are staying here.

QUICK: There's a fair bit of Oriel in you, Rose.
ROSE: Don't say that.
QUICK: Well, there's no telling you anything.

QUICK *heads out.*

SCENE 87

Evening. QUICK *patrols the neighbourhood.* SAM *finds* DOLLY *by the railway line, addled and frail.*

SAM: You keep wandering along that track, one of these days the eight-twelve's gonna collect you.

DOLLY: They go somewhere, the bastards. I always wanted to go somewhere. These rails go all over the world. They go forever.

SAM: Doll, what are you doin' here anyway? Better come home with me. Not safe out here like it used to be, eh?

He gets her up.

Hey, I won myself fifteen quid.

DOLLY: What on?

SAM: That mad bastard, the Monster. I bet he'd strike within the month.

DOLLY: You're a sick man.

SAM: It's common-sense. Anyone who kills that many has to like it. I bet he kills again this week.

DOLLY: You should be put down.

SAM: I'll take you to the flicks, eh?

DOLLY: I'm too old for the flicks. I should be drunk.

SAM: I should be rich. Well, come on, let's get home. I'm stranglin' for a cuppa.

DOLLY: I'll give him lollies.

SAM: Who, love?

DOLLY: Ted's boy. I thought he might be coming on the train.

SAM: Not tonight, Doll. Carn old girl, you're walkin' with a winner.

He leads her off.

DOLLY: I'd spoil him filthy if only he came to see his old grandma.

SCENE 88

LON *and* PANSY *at the centre of a* LAMB FAMILY *wedding.*

MINISTER'S VOICE: Do you, Logan Fitzwilliam Bruce Lamb, take this Pansy Maree Mullet to be your lawfully wedded wife?

ORIEL: He does.

PANSY: I never knew your name was Logan!

MINISTER'S VOICE: You may now kiss the bride.

LESTER: Welcome to the family, Pansy.

PANSY: I've already got a family, thanks. What I'd like is a decent honeymoon.

LON: I told you, we can't afford it.

> PANSY *is led into the house by* LON.

LESTER: Let me help you with these.

> LESTER *takes the bags.* RED *and* ELAINE *go.*

PANSY: Lon Lamb, this house gives me the willies. I never should have let you near me.

LON: Give it a rest, Pansy. At least you'll be safe here. The [Nedlands] Monster'd think twice before he had a crack at Cloudstreet. Don't you reckon?

> *They go.* PANSY *tosses her bouquet to* ELAINE. RED *catches it.*

SCENE 89

Night. A torch lights QUICK'*s patrol. Gunshots.* QUICK *rushes towards the sound.*

QUICK: Stop! Anybody there!? Stop. Police! Hello... I'm a Police Officer... [*He reaches down. His hands are covered in blood.*] Help! Help! [*He calls towards the caravan.*] Rose!

> ROSE *feels alone. She is now visibly pregnant.*

ROSE: Quick? Quick!

SCENE 90

Cloudstreet is dark. FISH *chants softly, growing louder.*

FISH: Quick and Rose. Quick and Rose. Quick and Rose!

> LESTER *finds* FISH.

LESTER: Mate. Fish! They're not here, mate. It's just a dream.

FISH: Quick and Rose. Coming. Coming home.

LESTER: They have their own home now, Fish.

FISH: Quick and Rose.

> ORIEL *emerges, followed by* LON *and* PANSY *and the rest of the house.* FISH *keeps calling.*

LON: Will you cut out the bloody noise? Some of us work round here.

PANSY: Enough said, we want bed.

ELAINE: Fish, go to bed...

> SAM *and* DOLLY *emerge.*

SAM: God Almighty, we thought someone was being murdered.

LESTER: Come on, boy, back to bed.

> ROSE *leads* QUICK *in.*

FISH: Quick and Rose!

ROSE: Got a spare bunk? Just for a week or two?

LESTER: What? Have you come to stay?

DOLLY / SAM: Stay as long as you like. [etc.]

QUICK: It seemed to make sense.

ROSE: I wasn't worried, mind you. Quick insisted. Said it wasn't safe.

FISH: Aarr! Quick and Rose! Aarrr!

ORIEL: No more talk. Lester, take their bags. We'll put a bed in the piano room.

ROSE: But, I wouldn't want to— [sleep there]

ORIEL: It's the only place big enough for a cot, Rose.

ROSE: But we're only staying till they catch the—

ORIEL: We can always brighten it up for you. Put a window in, even.

QUICK: We're not stayin' that long, Mum.

ORIEL: We'll see.

> ROSE *glances at* QUICK *as* ORIEL *and* LESTER *leave.*

DOLLY: Won't this be something', Rosie? We got a lot of catchin' up to do.

ROSE: Yeah, beauty.

> DOLLY *and* SAM *go.*

QUICK: Don't say it.

ROSE: I'll say one thing. I'm having this baby in hospital. All right?

FISH *whispers in* QUICK's *ear.*

QUICK: Rosie? Fish wants to feel the baby.

ROSE: Come on, mate. Hands on.

FISH *puts his hands on her belly.*

FISH: He's in there?

ROSE: That's what the doctors say. You could fool me.

FISH: The ladies won't like it.

ROSE: They'll get used to being grannies.

QUICK: Happy, Rose?

ROSE: It could be worse. We have a roof over our heads, even if it is the same old roof.

SCENE 91

LESTER: As summer turns to autumn, Lester watches Pansy and Rose swell to the finish line, racing each other to see who'll drop first. Lester looks forward to it. He misses having kids around. Kids to fool with and muck about with. Lester is somebody with kids. They believe in him. He makes them laugh. He can't make Quick laugh. Quick's falling back to the boy he was. He feels the sadness coming on him again. He's getting helpless, like the Quick Lamb of old. When the murderer kills again Quick feels he's responsible. He's dog-tired and doing double patrols. Still, there's something out there doing evil and he can't stop it.

Cloudstreet kitchen. QUICK *comes in from patrol.* LON *and heavily pregnant* PANSY *don't notice him at first.*

LON: When they got there, her body was still on the sofa. Hole right between the eyes.

PANSY: No.

LON: Just five streets from here. She was a babysitter. The kiddie was still asleep when the parents got home.

PANSY: Thank God for that.

LON: They reckon he raped her.

PANSY: Oh, no!

LON: That's right, isn't it, Quick? Nightie up around her chin.

PANSY: No.

LON: Yeah. Just sixteen. [*To* QUICK] You bludgers ever going to find him?

QUICK: What?

PANSY: Isn't it meant to be your job, catchin' criminals?

LESTER: Pansy, Lon...

LON: Well, this one's laughin', mate. What are you goin' to do? Wait till he leaves his address and phone number?

QUICK *bolts out of the house.*

SCENE 92

QUICK *angrily kicks objects round the yard.* FISH *watches.*

FISH: You want to play footie? Quick?

QUICK: No, Fish. Not right now.

FISH: Don't cry. The ladies like it.

QUICK: Get back inside, mate. Leave me alone, all right? I can't stop him. I can only clean up after him.

FISH: Like you clean up after me, Quick?

QUICK: No, not like that at all. Go back inside, mate. I'm all right.

FISH *passes* LESTER *as he goes.*

I'm going to throw it in, Dad.

LESTER: What?

QUICK: The war against evil, all that caper. The bastard's got me beaten. He's here to stay. He's going to be hanging over me from here on in.

LESTER: What would you do instead?

QUICK: I can drive trucks. Maybe I'll ask for a transfer to Traffic.

Quiet. Then an ear-splitting scream from the house.

Crikey, what now?

PANSY *comes out, followed by* LON.

PANSY: It's Rose! She's having the baby!

QUICK: Oh my God, Rose made me promise to take her to hospital.

LESTER: I'll get the truck started.

LON: No, I'll start the Harley! She can go in the sidecar!

ELAINE *runs out.*

ELAINE: It's too late! Come in, quick.

SCENE 93

LESTER, QUICK, ELAINE, PANSY *and* LON *hurry in to join* ELAINE *and* ORIEL *with* ROSE. FISH *arrives.*

ORIEL: She's getting close. Hot water, towels and a laundry bucket!

> ELAINE *runs for them.* ROSE *groans.*

Go easy, love, you'll tear your insides out. Fish, go to your room.
FISH: No.
QUICK: She all right?
LESTER: Orry's got it all under control.
ORIEL: She's fine. She's just having a baby.

> PANSY *stares at* ROSE *in horror.* SAM *arrives.*

SAM: What is it? Fire?
LESTER: Baby.
SAM: Oh, Gawd. Dolly's out to it.
ORIEL: Good Lord who made us, there's the head. No shouting. We'll frighten the creature. Here we come!

> *The* GHOSTS *retreat.* ROSE *sees them go.*

BLACK MAN: The room goes quiet. Two spirits, two strange women, one white and old, one black and young, are fading, fading, finally sent on their way to oblivion, free of the house, freeing the house, leaving a warm clean space among the living. The families circle round Rose like a two-up game. And the room sighs, the house breathes its first painless breath in half a century.
ROSE: They're fading. They're fading.
ORIEL: Who? Get the cord, Quick, take the cord.
QUICK: Gawd, he's got his fingers crossed.
ALL: Ahhhh!
ROSE: You mean it's a boy?
ORIEL: Wait a sec, love, we don't—
QUICK: He's all there, all right.
SAM: Don't worry, we all are, too.
ROSE: Haah!

> *The baby is held up.*

FISH: Look at that.

ORIEL: Fish, cut it out!

FISH: He's lookin' at me.

ROSE: Give him here, give him here.

ORIEL: Cover her up.

ROSE: Oh, the hell with it, now you've all seen me bits.

LESTER: Thank God, thank God, thank God.

ROSE: He's perfect, and he's gonna have sisters.

ORIEL: Pass the bucket, Elaine.

SAM: You're not puttin' him in the bucket?

ORIEL: She's got a placenta to come, you ignorant man.

SAM: Wish Dolly could have seen it.

ROSE: Shut up, Dad, and give me a kiss.

QUICK: After me.

They kiss her.

ELAINE: Don't get slushy.

LESTER: Red should've been here, she's the nurse.

ELAINE: No, she hates people's bits.

LESTER: She'll be dark on us for doin' it without her. She hates to miss out.

PANSY: I don't reckon I can go through with it.

ELAINE: Should have thought of that when you were goin' through with something else.

ORIEL: Make a pot, love. And get the girl a drink.

ROSE: He's hungry.

FISH: He's lookin' at me. He knows me. He loves me.

QUICK: We'll call him Harry.

ROSE: Not on your life.

QUICK: Look at the little larrikin. He's a home-built Harry if ever I saw one.

ROSE: Hold him, Quick, while I...

QUICK: What? I can't... I don't know.

ORIEL: Take him, you useless drongo.

QUICK *takes the baby.* ELAINE *sees the placenta.*

ELAINE: Oooer, what's that?

ORIEL: And to think we were blessed farmers!

QUICK: He's waxy!

111

LESTER: Wax Harry.

> CHUB *arrives.*

CHUB: Hey, guess what?

SAM: You're an uncle, Chub.

CHUB: Oh, yeah? Hey, you heard the news? They've caught him. A quiet little bloke called Cooke, with kids of his own. You hear me? They've got the Nedlands Monster!

SAM: Well, there you go.

FISH: Wax Harry.

ORIEL: Don't be ridiculous.

> DOLLY *appears, unnoticed.*

DOLLY: Is it alive?

ROSE: Yes. It's a boy.

DOLLY: Well, you can all just go and leave her alone. I'm a grandmother. Good night.

> *They leave* DOLLY *with* ROSE *and the baby.*

SCENE 94

FISH *is alone outside the house.*

BLACK MAN: There it is, Fish, your gift to them, the man, the woman, the baby, a gift bought with pain and shortening. Soon you'll be a man, Fish, though only for a moment. Long enough to see, smell, touch, hear, taste the muted glory of wholeness, and finish what was begun only a moment ago down there where the light is outswinging on the water and your brother is laughing. The earth slips away, Fish, and soon, soon you'll be yourself. Soon, but not yet.

SCENE 95

LON: The Nedlands Monster comes to trial, and the city stinks of happiness. The Monster gets the hangman's noose and everyone goes wild with excitement.

> *Cloudstreet.* ROSE *feeds the baby.* QUICK *has a newspaper.*

Whacko! They gave him death. They're going to hang the
Monster.

ROSE: Good riddance.

QUICK: Thank God for that.

ORIEL: Leave God out of it. Killing is men's business, not God's.

QUICK: You never saw what he did, Mum. They didn't call him a
monster for nothin'.

LESTER: He's only a man, son.

ORIEL: And other men have got no right—

QUICK: What about an eye for an eye and a tooth for a tooth?

ORIEL: Barbarism! That's for primitive tribes.

QUICK: That's the Bible, Mum. Your old inspiration. And don't
pretend you've given it away. I've seen you out there with it,
burnin' the midnight candle. Readin' bits over and over again,
out there where no one can see you. You go and read the bits
about justice.

ORIEL *can't reply, and runs away.*

What was all that about?

LESTER: Principles, Quick.

QUICK: Mum's principles are work, work and work.

LESTER: You don't understand what she works at, do you?

QUICK: Obviously not.

LESTER *takes out a little book, reads...*

LESTER: 'Master, which is the greatest commandment in the law?
Jesus said unto him, thou shalt love the Lord thy God with all
thy heart, and with all thy soul, and with all thy mind. This is the
first commandment. And the second is like unto it. Thou shalt
love thy neighbour as thyself.'

QUICK: It's from another time. She doesn't even believe it.

LESTER: She tries. That's her work.

QUICK: But she can't love the Lord. Not since Fish. She can't!

LESTER: But she tries, Quick. Can't you see?

LESTER *goes.*

QUICK: I can see. She can't. The bastard's better off dead.

113

SCENE 96

QUICK: Then one day, Quick's eating his sandwich by the river when he sees a child, face down, a floater on the incoming tide. Boots socks trousers and all, Quick slams into the water. When he gets to the facedown body, he hoists him over and finds he's about an hour late to save a life. The child's skin is already doughy, his clouded eyes look up at the sky, and Quick has to cover the boy's face with his own hands. The sight sets off too many thoughts. But Quick forces himself to take his hands away and see it for what it really is. It's Wax Harry's face. It's his own boyhood face. It's his brother's face. Fish. It's the sight of the world ending, someone's son dead. 'It's my life all over again', thinks Quick. 'This will always be happening.'

SARGE *appears.*

SARGE: You won't believe who that is, Lamb. That's whatsisname's kid. The Monster. Been missing since this morning.

QUICK: Quick feels something break in him and he stares at his boots. The poor bastard, the poor, poor bastard, sitting down there in Freo gaol waiting for the hangman, thinking there's no news worse than he's heard, and now this is heading his way.

SARGE *goes.* ROSE *appears.*

ROSE: What's up? Why are you looking like that?

QUICK: We all turn into the same thing, don't we? There's no them. It's us, Rose, us and us and us. We all join up somewhere in the end.

ROSE: Join up with who? What do you mean?

QUICK: The gaols are full of blokes we'd swear are different from us. Only difference is, they did things you and me just thought about.

ROSE: That's a fair difference.

QUICK: A second's difference. I could have turned out like him. Angry and cold, I can see how that evil little bugger might have just turned like a pot of milk.

SCENE 97

SAM *is on his way out. He gets out a cigarette. The* BLACK MAN *lights his fag.*

SAM: Ta. Just off to vote. You got yours in?

    The BLACK MAN *laughs.*

    Not that it's much use. It's a boss's country straight up.

BLACK MAN: Only the bosses don't know they're the bosses, eh? You live there.

SAM: Yeah, I own it.

BLACK MAN: You shouldn't break a place. Places are strong.

SAM: Eh?

BLACK MAN: Too many places busted. You better be the strongest man.

SAM: What are you talkin' about!

    The BLACK MAN *laughs and moves on.*

SCENE 98

The LAMB *side of Cloudstreet.* ROSE, *Harry and all the* LAMBS *are there.* PANSY *nurses her baby, Merrilyn Gaye. The* PICKLES *family arrive.*

ORIEL: Come in, come in!

LESTER: Welcome below deck!

ROSE: Sit down, Mum and Dad.

ORIEL: Mr Pickles—

SAM: Call me Sam, why don't you?

ORIEL: I believe you've got something to say to us all, Sam.

SAM: You never were a dawdler, Mrs Lamb.

ORIEL: Oriel.

SAM: Oriel. I'm thinkin'... Oriel, Lest... I'm thinkin' we might have had the best of this place.

LESTER: How do you mean?

SAM: Well...

DOLLY: Spit it out, Sam. He's thinkin' of sellin' up. A present from his Cousin Joel and he wants to sell it!

SAM: Shut up, Doll, you hate the place.

DOLLY: Joel bought it with his winnings off a horse. What do they say about lookin' a gift horse in the mouth, Sam?

SAM: I said shut up, woman! They're goin' mad in this town, Lest, buyin' the old, and buildin' the new. I want to do what Rose and

Quick have done. Build a new house, out in a new suburb. [*To* ORIEL *and* LESTER] I suppose youse are worried about your position.

DOLLY: They are paid up on rent till about Harry's twentieth birthday, you silly coot. We'd have to pay 'em to leave.

ORIEL: If we have to leave, there's nothin' to be done. It's only a house.

SAM: I expect it'd be more wiser to buy your own by now.

ORIEL: No, no, it does you good to be tenants. It reminds you of your own true position in the world. A house should be a home, a privilege, not a possession. It's foolish to get attached.

SAM: Fair enough.

ORIEL: But I have got used to it here. You might say I've come to love this awful old house. It never made it easy for us, and there've been times I've thought the place has been trying to itch us out. But I reckon we've made our mark on it now. We're halfway to belonging here, and I don't know where I'd go any more. Out there, they're bulldozing streets and old places, filling in the river, like they don't want to leave any traces behind. I reckon Harry and Merrilyn Gaye will never see the places we know. Can you imagine that? What am I gunna do, walk out into that? This place has been good to me.

DOLLY: She's right. You're right, Oriel. The bloody place has got to us.

QUICK: Good on you, Doll.

LESTER: It's twenty years, soon. Twenty years.

SAM: Yeah, and Joel said I could sell after twenty. I'll do all right out of it, too. Some rich bastard'll come along, bulldoze it and build a bloody great block of flats on it. Salmon pink brick, five storeys, ugly as sin.

Silence.

Well, that's it, then. We stay.

LESTER: That's the way, Sam. You can't just break a place up.

SAM: That's what some Abo told me. He said I was piss-weak.

DOLLY: He was bloody well right.

ORIEL: Remember which side of the corridor you're on. The language!

ELAINE: More tea?

LESTER: Yes. A toast.

SAM: What to?

LESTER: To us. And this old place. We're all stayin'.

ROSE *glances at* QUICK.

QUICK: We're not staying. Our house is ready, and soon as we come back from holidays we'll be moving in there.

DOLLY: Well, the rest of us are staying. Aren't we? Chub's staying.

CHUB *nods, and eats.*

LON: We're staying.

PANSY *grimaces.*

RED: I'm staying. And Elaine's staying.

ELAINE: For the time being.

LESTER: To the stayers. To Cloudstreet. Now we'd better have a song. Somethin' to mark the occasion.

DOLLY: What, the national bloody anthem?

SAM: No, nothin' royalist here. We'll have an Australian song.

LESTER: They're all Irish!

They sing. QUICK *and* ROSE *take Harry and slide out.*

SCENE 99

FISH *catches them leaving.*

FISH: Quick? Quick? Me, too, Quick.

QUICK: No.

FISH: I wanna go.

QUICK: No, Fish.

FISH: I wanna.

QUICK: You can't, mate. This is just for me and Rose and Harry.

FISH: And me!

QUICK: No, Fish. Get back inside.

FISH: Please is the magic word.

ROSE: Get him packed.

QUICK: What?

ROSE: Get him packed before I change my mind.

QUICK: I'll wait till you do.

ROSE: If he wants to come, let him come.

QUICK: Rose, we've already got Harry to think of. Fish is a big retarded bloke and he'll cause no end of—

ROSE: Listen to yourself. It's Fish, for God's sake.

FISH: Yeah.

QUICK: Mum'll never let him go.

ROSE: You still afraid of your mother?

FISH: Yeah!

ROSE: If he doesn't come, we'll both drive out of here feeling like a pair of right bastards. They'll have to lock him in his room and you'll go dark on me for a week. I want a good time. I've brought *Anna Karenina* and I want to lie back somewhere feeding Harry with you reading it to us. Fish'll like that, too. He's always game for a story. Go and tell them.

QUICK: The things a man does when he's in love.

ROSE: There's worse yet, Quick Lamb. I've got other demands.

> QUICK *goes inside.* ROSE *surveys* FISH *on the bags.*

Oh, Fish.

FISH: Oh, Rose Pickles.

ROSE: I always said I'd take you away with me. And now we're off. But where to?

FISH: The water. Hurry, Quick, the water.

> QUICK *brings a bag for* FISH. *They board the truck.*

SCENE 100

BLACK MAN: They head out through bald, silent wheat towns... Cunderdin, Kellerberrin, Merredin, Bodallin, inland beyond rivers, beyond rain and pleasure, out to where they're homeless, where they've never belonged. Fish is asleep on the back seat. Dust and pollen settle on the upholstery. They drive on till nightfall.

> ROSE, QUICK, FISH *and Harry on the road.*

FISH: I need a poo.

QUICK: Just wait a little while, mate.

FISH: Quick.

QUICK: Hang on, we're lookin' for a place to camp.

ROSE: And generally being aimless and dithery. Are we there yet?

QUICK: Where?

ROSE: Wherever we're going.

FISH *moans.*

QUICK: What's that bloody smell?

FISH: I told you, Quick. But I told!

QUICK: Oh, fuck a duck, he's shat himself. Now what?

ROSE: Now you hop out and clean him up.

QUICK: Come on, Fish. Stop blubberin'. Hop out.

BLACK MAN: Quick kneels to take down Fish's trousers. He sees the white rolls of fat, the ramshackle patchwork of his undies, and it's not a body he recognises. Fish turns his head aside in shame as Quick slides the shorts off. He gags a moment and slings them into the ditch, glad his mother isn't there to see the wanton waste. The size of Fish, the stubbornness of shit in the black hair of him, the thought of how they've come to this threatens to break something in Quick's throat. Against the back fender Fish's whole putty body is jerking. His buttocks shiver while Quick hugs his legs, as the wheat bends a moment to the breeze that has sprung out of the very earth itself.

QUICK *has changed* FISH. FISH *and Harry go to sleep.*

ROSE: Tell you a secret. You won't believe this.

QUICK: Try me.

ROSE: I can't bear to think of any of us leaving Cloudstreet. We belong to it, Quick, and I want to stay.

QUICK: You're havin' me on.

ROSE: Must be Sam's old Shifty Shadow. I spend years trying to escape, and end up married to a Lamb, back in the thick of it.

QUICK: But what about our place? After all that trouble? Our own place!

ROSE: I don't know about our own place. I like the old place, the crowds and the noise. And, well… I suppose I like the idea, it's like getting another childhood, another go at things. I'm back in the old house with the boy next door and his baby, and I'm not miserable or starving or frightened. I'm right in the middle. It's like a village. I have these feelings. I can never explain these feelings.

QUICK: But you hate family stuff.

ROSE: But it's two families. It's a new tribe.

QUICK: Don't you want to be independent?

ROSE: I don't know what that means anymore. If it means being alone, I don't want it. If I was gunna be independent, do you think I'd need a husband? And a kid? And a mother and father, and in-laws and friends and neighbours? When I want to be independent, I retire. I go skinny and puke. I begin to disappear. But I want to live, I want to be with people, Quick. I want to battle it out. I don't want our new house. I want the life I have. Don't be disappointed.

QUICK: Disappointed? Love, I'm putrid with... with happiness. I've been wantin' to say that for months.

ROSE: You big drongo! Why did they call you Quick? I never knew.

QUICK: Come on. I told you plenty of times.

ROSE: No, you never did.

QUICK: They called me Quick... 'cause I'm the slowest bastard that ever lived.

She laughs. They kiss, then sleep.

BLACK MAN: Quick curls into Fish on one side and Rose with Wax Harry settles in on the other. Above them the black sky looks crisp with stars. Dots as worlds, and milky smears as worlds of worlds. In the deep night, Quick wakes with the moon white on his face. Fish is awake beside him, kissing him on the cheek. The moon is all over his face, or it seems to be until Quick sees the light is coming off Fish himself. There's a long steady rustling in the wheat, rhythmic as the sound of sleep. Quick thinks of a herd of roos grazing, but it comes closer, and is too musical to ignore. He sees a line of figures moving between the trees.

He shakes Rose awake and sees the black widen in her eyes. They see children, naked children, rising from the ground like a mineral spring, faces, arms, eyes and legs travelling in eddies, passing them with the lapping sound of feet.

Nobody speaks, not even Wax Harry. The tide of naked children swirls around them until the stars are low enough to touch their eyes heavy, and the great adventure of sleep takes them back while the children part the wheat like the wind itself and take all night to pass.

SCENE 101

QUICK, ROSE, *Harry and* FISH *arrive back at Cloudstreet. Early morning.* ELAINE *is opening up the shop.*

ELAINE: You're not due home.

QUICK: Get up, all of youse.

> *The* PARENTS *come out of the house.*

We're having a picnic. To celebrate.

SAM: What picnic? Celebrate what?

ORIEL: What's this foolishness? It's Wednesday morning, work to be done.

SAM: They're celebratin'.

QUICK: No, all of us.

DOLLY: God, I've never been up this early unless I never went to bed.

LESTER: What are we celebratin'?

ROSE: We're stayin'.

LESTER: No, we're stayin'.

ORIEL: You're stayin'?

ROSE: We're all stayin'! For as long as it takes.

ORIEL: To do what?

ROSE: To get old and die. To count the angels on the head of a pin, I dunno. A day, a week, a Test Match, a session of Parliament, a decade, I dunno. Till the bloody walls come down, Oriel!

LESTER: Picnic, you reckon?

DOLLY: I'll get my hat.

SAM: What the hell.

ORIEL: Don't stand there, youse bludgers. Pack the truck, lock the shop, grab a hamper. Let's go to the river. Let's do it right, for once!

> *Both families race for the river. Music.*

SCENE 102

Riverbank. The LAMB *and* PICKLES *families make their picnic. The* BLACK MAN *is there.* FISH *watches, then heads for the water.* QUICK *might stop him, but lets him go.*

FISH: I know my story for just long enough to see how we've come, how we've all battled in the same corridor that time makes for us, and I'm Fish Lamb for those seconds it takes to die, as long as it takes to drink the river, as long as it took to tell you all this, and then my walls are tipping and I burst into the moon, sun and stars of who I truly am. Being Fish Lamb. Perfectly. Always. Everyplace. Me.

He's gone into the water. QUICK *lets him go.*

CURTAIN